TH

Dr. Stua an inter known writer and authority on Jewish life and culture. He combines an impressive scholarly background with the awareness and concern of a religious leader very much involved in the great contemporary issues of faith. He is Senior Rabbi of Beth Tzedec Congregation in Toronto, one of Canada's largest synagogues.

TO UNDERSTAND JEWS

Stuart E. Rosenberg

HODDER AND STOUGHTON
LONDON · SYDNEY · AUCKLAND · TORONTO

Contents

PART THREE

The Jewish Life:
From Cradle to Grave

EPILOGUE

Introduction

Are Jews only a fraction of a large, cosmopolitan population in the Western world, a slight statistic in a massive total? If they are only that, how do we account for the tremendous interest in them that we can find in almost every day's newspaper, and most especially since the rise of the modern State of Israel?

The fact is that, while Jews do not figure significantly in the "numbers game" of civilization, deep down every intelligent Christian and Muslim knows that without Judaism there could be neither Christianity nor Islam. More than all else, this explains the conscious (and often unconscious) spiritual need of those who are not of their faith, culture, or history to understand the Jews.

But it was not until the beginnings of Christian ecumenism that many Christians began to express this need openly, and to confess publicly their almost total lack of knowledge of Jews and of Judaism. Without doubt the greatest single force for this open philo-Semitism was the late, lamented, and saintly Pope John XXIII. Perhaps this prayer that he composed shortly before his death tells more than a score of lectures could tell about the essential drive that has made it necessary for Christians to come to know their Jewish brothers in a new way:

"We realize now that many, many centuries of blindness have dimmed our eyes, so that we no longer see the beauty of Thy Chosen People and no longer recognize in their faces the features of our first-born brother. We realize that our brows are branded with the mark of

Cain. Centuries long has Abel lain in blood and tears, because we had forgotten Thy Love. Forgive us the curse which we unjustly laid on the name of the Jews. Forgive us that, with our curse, we crucified Thee a second time."

And if Pope John could speak of the Jews out of the fullness of the religious need to come to terms with history, and to place the Jews back once more into the mainstream of Christian love and thought, there was another man in high place, Prime Minister Pierre Trudeau of Canada, who saw the need to understand Jews from still another angle of vision. "The truth is," he said, "that having been chosen, the Jews are destined to remain a minority amongst the peoples of the world." But what kind of minority? And why so important for the majority? Because, Mr. Trudeau went on, "they are in fact the quintessence of a minority."

Perhaps, here, we have the fuller, more contemporary reason for the urgency many feel about getting to know more about their Jewish neighbours, to come to terms with the capacity of the Jews to stand apart these many centuries in spite of persecution and intolerance. Not only are they a minority, but as "the quintessence of a minority" they have provided lessons from their ability to survive every calamity – even Hitler's holocaust – that may very well give strength and spiritual guidance to all minorities.

And what, then, is a majority, after all, if not the sum total of all minorities?

It is for that larger majority, the sum of all minorities, that this book about the Jews – their peoplehood, their culture, and their religion – is intended.

Dr. Stuart E. Rosenberg
Maple, Ontario
Passover, April 1972

PART ONE
The Growth of Judaism

I

"Spiritually, We Are All Semites"

One of the most heartening aspects of the contemporary ecumenical movement is that its leading spokesmen are scholars who are pointing the way toward new relations among the religions—through patient investigation of the historical and theological sources. They have made clear that in order to prepare for wise, mutual accommodations in the future, the unprejudiced study of the past becomes a moral imperative. As a result, Christians are rethinking their earlier days as never before, seeking out a history they had often allowed themselves to forget, redressing incorrect interpretations they had refused to uproot.

As part of this exciting effort to know the whole truth about themselves, many Christians are discovering for the first time their need to begin at their beginning—with Judaism. While the cast of their thinking is clearly molded of a desire to arrive at a *more scholarly and intelligent understanding of Christianity*, these efforts must surely lead Christians to a *new awareness and appreciation of Judaism*. What once seemed like a fossil can now come alive; it becomes relevant, vital and significant. Christians can now discover for themselves the profound implications of the truth spoken by the late Pope Pius XI, when he declared: "Spiritually, we are all Semites."

Yet, like many another truth, this religious formulation is often consigned by the uninformed to the scrap-heap of oblivion. Many Christians, of course, know that Jesus was a Jew, yet, somehow, they feel that Judaism really played no part in his life, since he was a "Christian"! This helps to explain the tremendous gap that exists in their religious education—a gap that not only creates problems in self-understanding, but that also leads to perpetuation of group barriers. For if these people had been properly taught, they would know what every Christian scholar knows: *"Jesus was a son of the covenant and behaved as an ardently religious, practicing Jew."*

Henri Daniel-Rops, the distinguished French Catholic scholar who was responsible for that particular quotation, also made it clear why no Christian can truly understand his own religion, unless he also understands the Judaism which Jesus practiced. He wrote: "When he began his ministry, in what context did he do so, and who were his helpers, his collaborators? The physical context was that of the Jewish land, that Palestine which he practically never left in all his many journeys. His disciples, the twelve apostles, were all Jews, most of them peasants and fishermen from Galilee: their names alone show this—Simon, John, Jude and Judas, Levi, who was to be Matthew, and the others. When he spoke, his style was so impregnated with the Jewish manner of expression that the rhythms, the balanced repetitions and alliterations of Hebrew poetry are to be felt even in the Greek of the gospels, just as in his parables we are aware of the same manner of thought as that which produced the *midrash* (the Rabbinic literature) of Israel. . . .

". . . But it was not only by birth, breeding, manner of life, friendship and means of expression that Jesus, as a man, was a Jew and so wholly a Jew. . . . He was also a Jew in that he recognized that his people had a particular mission and a destiny entirely of their own. He, like all his countrymen, was a son of the covenant." (See Henri Daniel-Rops, *Daily Life in the Time of Jesus,* New York, 1962, pp. 481-3).

This is a secular age, and more than ever, those who believe need to stand together. In itself, this need has the power to produce new religious discoveries. One such discovery is the Christian rediscovery of roots that are Semitic. The stronger a Christian's faith, the more profoundly it permeates his life, that more "Semitic" a Christian will know himself to be.

This is a teaching suggested by Father Thurston Davis, S.J., editor of the Catholic weekly, *America.* The world needs them both, he reminds both Catholics and Jews. Says he: "Catholics or Jews, we *can't* vanish. We have to be ourselves, true to our traditions, until the day when in God's good time he brings us together at last. . . . Unvanishing, unwilling to vanish, in combined strength we must labor. . . . We have so much to do together for the common good. . . . Side by side, before we vanish, let's get some of this work done."

This is the spirit in which this book has been written. In the ardent wish that it will lead to respectful and humane Christian-Jewish encounters, we now embark on what one hopes can be a fruitful voyage of spiritual discovery.

II

Biblical Judaism

The Hebrew Bible was not buried in the ruins of the ages, nor covered by the sands of history. Virtually alone among the literatures of ancient cultures it survived the silt of time's deluge. It has emerged from antiquity as a unique, protected record of the earlier epochs.

We take it so much for granted that we fail to realize how poorly the literature written during the same period by the nations surrounding Israel has fared. The writings of Mesopotamia remained buried under the dusty ruins of half-forgotten cities—Ur of the Chaldees, Nineveh and Babylon. Only the spades of recent excavators could bring the libraries of Babylonia, in the form of clay tablets, to life again, and then only for the student of antiquities.

Even the cultural treasures of Egypt, preserved in its dry open sunlight, continue to be regarded as alien and esoteric relics of an older day. For men had forgotten how to read the language of the people of the Nile, and not until a century ago was a linguistic key discovered to unlock the code. Obviously, whatever was great and valuable in that literature could not have had any impact upon the growth of civilization. Today, only the rare student—the Egyptologist, as he is called—has direct access to its teachings and insights.

In the face of man's normal forgetfulness of his past, how could this miracle of history have occurred?

The men of ancient Israel who were responsible for the authoring and editing of Scripture viewed their task in a way quite dissimilar from their pagan contemporaries. They believed that what they wrote or gathered together derived from the one true God who entered into a unique covenant with their people, Israel. This pact, or *b'rith,* had specific terms of reference: God loved and protected Israel because Israel worshipped no other God but him, and voluntarily agreed to accept his law.

Unless we take this religious factor into serious account, the very touchstone by which the unbroken tradition of the Hebrew Bible must be measured will be lost. Those who sheltered and protected this literature as a living Scripture—the people of Israel—kept it as a holy book, preserved its language as a holy language, regarded the land of its birth as the Holy Land, called its significant sites holy places, and understood the history it records as universal because it was sacred and redemptive history. This explains why it has come down to us, if not completely intact, then surely as the most comprehensive summary of the culture of a people ever to be safeguarded by so few, for so many, for so long.

There are sagas of families, biographies of heroes, proverbs, chronicles, poems, prophecies, philosophical tracts, a novelette, love-songs and verse-play in the Hebrew Bible. But arching over and running through them like a silver cord is the central, crucial theme: God in the life of man And if we have this sacred library in our hands today it is because the congregations of Israel saw themselves as God's people who were covenanted to him to retell his story. For this reason, Jews do not regard Hebrew Scripture as an "Old Testament"; their compact with God remains, indeed can never be broken, unless *they* willfully discard it. For Jews, their "old" testament remains as an ever "new" testament.

The Hebrew Bible is divided into three parts: the Torah, or Pentateuch, also known as the Five Books of Moses; the Prophets, Former and Latter, major and minor; and the general miscellany, called The Writings, or Hagiographa. These books comprise a veritable library, and their titles follow:

I.	II.	III.
Pentateuch	*The Prophets*	*The Writings*
Genesis	(Former)	Psalms
Exodus	Joshua	Proverbs
Leviticus	Judges	Job
Numbers	I Samuel	Song of Songs
Deuteronomy	II Samuel　　*The*	Ruth
	I Kings　　*Five*	Lamentations
	II Kings　　*Scrolls*	Ecclesiastes
		Esther
	(Latter)	Daniel
	The	Ezra
	Major Prophets	Nehemiah
	Isaiah	I Chronicles
	Jeremiah	II Chronicles
	Ezekiel	

I.	II.	III.
	The Minor Prophets	

Hosea ⎫
Joel
Amos
Obadiah
Jonah
Micah
Nahum   *The Twelve*
Habakkuk
Zephaniah
Haggai
Zechariah
Malachi ⎭

The Biblical Religion of Israel

The religion of Israel as depicted in the Hebrew Bible must first be approached in terms of its context: how did it differ from pagan thought? The pagan religions deified nature and thus came to regard as their personal gods the various elements in nature. Pagans believed that these gods were connected to the processes of nature, as persons. Thus when men, in those days, looked at lightning and thunder, the sun and the rain, they thought of them as personal deities who, like men, were born, were married, had children, engaged in battles, died, and were often resurrected. Indeed, these biographies of the gods—the stories of their birth, life and death—constitute the sum and substance of pagan mythology.

These mythologies—the pagan "Scriptures"—are most revealing. They show the limitations of the gods who are themselves the creation of primeval forces, older and more powerful than they. Thus, these gods of the ancients had neither independent divine will nor ultimate power. Omnipotent, unknown and unknowable powers placed the entire pagan world—men and their gods, alike—in the tight grip of a blind fate that was irrational, amoral and inescapable. The gods might employ magic in an attempt to make these occult forces do their bidding. Men, following in this way, did not really worship their gods, but rather participated in a magical cult whose rites, it was supposed, could change the course of nature, *i.e.,* could bring the rains or make them stop. Ultimately, however, neither the magic of men nor the powers of their gods could change the fates which enthralled them both—fates imposed by mysterious, primeval forces.

Over against this world of static, helpless paganism, the people of Israel held a view of man and God that had no parallel. Indeed, the very uniqueness of their life-style was the result of their consciousness of a God who had singled them out from among the nations. He had elected them as his people, to remain undefiled by the immoralities of pagan life. Israel's God, Yahweh, rules the universe with an intelligence directed by moral purposes. He is free to act, and man, whom he created in his image, mirrors the divine freedom. Men may choose: life or death, good or evil, the blessing or the curse. Indeed, it is this very freedom that carries the seeds of man's undoing; it is both blessing and curse.

Pagan life was violent and immoral because pagans believed that the elements of nature—their gods—were locked in mortal, ongoing battle, ever in conflict. They did not know of the single Creator who structures his creation in harmony, order, and with moral purpose. In monotheistic Israel, such cosmological conflict—godly warfare in nature—was, of course, impossible. A serious conflict of another kind was known, however,

and, indeed, it forms the basis of biblical ethics and religion. This is the conflict of man with God, a struggle
that results from his freedom to choose to hearken to
God's word, or to rebel against it. Man does rebel—
this is his sin—and his rebellion is the source of the
world's evil. But he is not God's pawn; he may repent
and do what is good, because by his very nature he is a
moral creature who can freely respond to God's moral
law.

This is the special significance of two historical
events in the life of Israel which the Bible sees as
singularly related: the exodus from Egypt and the
Torah-revelation at Sinai. To be liberated from servitude is important, to be sure, for unfree men cannot
make moral choices. But the liberation of Israel from
human bondage was important primarily because of
what it made possible: the whole people could now become the servants of the Lord. At Sinai, the covenant
God had once sealed with individuals—Abraham,
Isaac and Jacob—he now makes with an entire community, all of their descendants. At Sinai, he gives
Israel his Torah—his teaching and law—and thereby
all of Israel becomes the people of God. "You shall be
unto me a kingdom of priests and a holy nation." By
placing Israel—and Israel alone—under the yoke of his
commandments, this people now stands apart from the
pagan world. The other nations remain tied to idolatry
and immoral ways. Only Israel knows God, for God
called Israel out of Egypt and made Israel his people
when he gave—and they received—his Torah.

"The Torah speaks in the language of men." This
teaching of the Rabbis suggests an important truth
Jews associate with a proper understanding of the
Bible. Of course, the Bible is revered and studied as the
word of God, but it must also be understood as the

work of man. God's word is heard by men, but men can grow in their knowledge of God: the Bible depicts not only a movement of God to man, but also a movement of man to God. Even the covenant is bilateral: God chose Israel, but Israel, collectively at Sinai, also chose God. As Israel grows in its knowledge of God, it also deepens its self-awareness as the people of the covenant. Thus, the meaning of the covenant may also grow. By the 8th century, some of the people were ready for a larger view of their role. In the name of the Lord, prophets arose who spoke and were heard. What were men like Isaiah, Amos, Hosea and Micah saying?

They wanted to reinstate the moral foundations of the covenant, eroded by the creeping paganism that, ever since Sinai, had been filtering into Israel's life in Canaan. In their bones burned a fiery passion to divorce Israel from an impossible marriage—the popular "religion" which had grown up, wherein the idolatrous orgiastic Syrian, Assyrian or Canaanitish cults were falsely wedded to the moral demands of Israel's covenant. Kings, even priests of Israel, had sometimes led the people astray. Among pagans, kings were made into gods and priests regarded as final authorities. But not for Israel, the prophets thundered. God alone is King and even the great mortal monarchs—even King David—are forever subject to his law. Nor may Israel's priests go unchallenged when they raise their paltry rituals to levels higher than God's moral demands; indeed, the holiness of God does not require the cult of priestly worship at shrine or temple. It is man who desires kings, man who needs worship, man who delights in the "noise of solemn assemblies."

God, the prophets emphasized, wants more—he requires justice and love! These are the attributes of his holiness and the people becomes a holy people when it imitates God. Poignantly, they make known God's true needs: "To what purpose is the multitude of your sacrifices unto me? . . . They are a burden unto me; I am weary to bear them . . . Wash you, make you clean. Put away the evil of your doings from before mine eyes. Cease to do evil; learn to do well; seek justice, relieve the oppressed; judge the fatherless, plead for the widow" (Isaiah 1, 11-17).

But even more than they wanted to elevate the covenant, the prophets sought to universalize it. They gave the covenant a new and a radical meaning. Idolatry, they now taught, was to be only a passing phase in human experience. History moves toward the universal acceptance of God's moral law, and Israel becomes the instrument of God's triumph and mankind's redemption.

The older religion had regarded monotheism as a universal experience only from the days of creation until the generation of the Tower of Babel. Thereafter, the nations reverted to idolatry, and it was believed that idolatry was to remain their eternal way of life. Only Israel was to be different, and the covenant was a sign of its uniqueness—chosen to serve as the lone monotheist among the nations. Now, however, the prophets endow Israel's covenant with a missionary meaning: Israel must persevere until the End of Days, when God will make himself known to all the nations, as he did to Israel.

If anything, Israel's religious burden as the chosen one now becomes heavier and more difficult. The people, to use Isaiah's phrase, must now be "a light unto the nations." To keep that light pure, the leaders of the people and the nation itself must give up every last trace of immorality. The prophets do not chastise them only for extraordinary immorality—like murder, robbery, or sexual sins—but for day-to-day sins; false scales, unfair prices, the undefended poor, the bribed priest or the corrupted judge. For sins such as these, the holy nation must be held accountable. If it does not repent of these evils, Israel will be overwhelmed by the heathen empires, will fall, and will be driven into exile.

But Israel will rise again, will be restored to and redeemed in Zion. The glory of her kingdom will be renewed and the beloved House of David returned. In that time, the king, or messiah (in Hebrew, "messiah" means "one who is anointed," or king) will lead his people in the spirit of wisdom and understanding. What, in the prophetic view, makes the messiah-king different from kings who came before? As ever in Israel, though he be king, he is only a man, and his ministrations must be performed in "the fear of the Lord." He is surely no god—in their eyes such a view would be pagan and blasphemous. Yet, he *is* different from all other kings of Israel: he, alone, will be capable of ruling his people in perfect conformity to the will and the word of God. Because of his unique spiritual endowments, his leadership creates the conditions necessary for the fulfillment of the covenant. Clearly, it is the covenant that preoccupies the prophets, more than all else. It is *Israel* as the "light unto the nations" that is central to their thought, not the person or powers of the messiah-king. From a restored, redeemed and purified Israel, secure in Zion, God's peace, love and justice will descend upon the whole world.

These hopeful views sustained the people when Israel fell, and later when Jerusalem was destroyed. They took these teachings of the prophets with them into exile, and the law and love of God went with them, too. In Babylonia, they sang of Zion and remembered the vision of their prophets. When, with

Ezra, they do return, they are eager to hear God's word, once more in Zion.

Now, the word becomes Torah—Sinai made eternal and universal—as it is reverently recorded and made into a Sacred Scripture that can be studied and taught anywhere, by Israel itself, or by those influenced by Israel. This was accomplished during Ezra's time, in the middle of the 5th century B.C., when the Five Books of Moses were edited. Some two hundred years later, the *Former Prophets* (actually historical books from the time of the conquest of Canaan until the fall of Jerusalem) and the *Latter Prophets* (the twelve "Minor Prophets" and the three "Major Prophets") were joined together to become the second part of accepted Scripture.

The last of the three sections of the Hebrew Bible, *The Writings,* came into the Scripture much later, at a convention of Rabbis, in Jamnia, about the year 100 of the Christian era. This section posed special difficulties because, by this time, various sects had grown up in Judaism, and some of the books which their followers regarded as sacred did not receive the official sanction of the Rabbis. The problem turned on the question of "divine inspiration." If a book was believed to have been written before "divine inspiration" had ceased to be revealed to men, it was judged sacred; if later, it was deemed unacceptable as Scripture. Many of those which never made their way into the Hebrew Bible were popular among Greek-speaking Jews of Alexandria, and did appear in their Greek translation, the *Septuagint.* Since the early Church was concerned, on the whole, with Greek-speaking pagans and Jews, it used the *Septuagint* as its Bible. This was indeed fortunate for, as a result, the Apocrypha, those books the Palestinian Rabbis had regarded as spurious, and which they hid in order to keep from becoming too popular, were saved for posterity by the Church which considered them to be canonical. In the Catholic version of the Bible, these books appear scattered throughout the Old Testament.

III

Rabbinic Judaism

Rabbinic Judaism saved biblical religion—for all men, and for all time.

Some people, unfortunately, have been mistakenly taught to believe that Judaism died spiritually 150 years before Christianity, when its biblical period came to an end. They assume that once the Hebrew Bible became the possession of the world through Christianity, the Jewish religion, then, and forever after, had nothing important to say or do.

What escapes their understanding is a simple fact of history: if Jewish religious creativity had indeed ended with the close of the Hebrew biblical era, nobody in the world—not even Jews, for too long thereafter—would know that testament. Indeed, much less could they have accepted its teachings. If it were not for Rabbinic Judaism, biblical religion would have become as strange, remote, and unknown to us as have all the other forgotten religions of the ancient Near East.

This is so because Rabbinic Judaism introduced a revolutionary and daring concept to the world—a missionary, proselytizing religion, with doors opened to the stranger. This new form of Judaism went far beyond anything the prophets taught, for in that older world, a people's religion and national culture were one and the same, and outsiders could not enter the closed society created by "ethnic religion." It was the post-biblical Jewish community, under the impact of its new teachers—the Rabbis of the Talmud—which was the first in history to reject the idea of a biologically-determined, nationally-autonomous society. It welcomed into the life of the nation as Jews, all who voluntarily accepted the Jewish religion, and granted them full equality with its native-born. Judaism was not just a "religion"; by accepting the faith one also became a member of the Jewish people.

Christianity grew up in the soil of Rabbinic Judaism. Its missionary zeal, which led ultimately to its acceptance as the religion of the Roman Empire, thus becoming a world religion, is the product of that nurture. Paradoxically, however, the universal religion of Judaism did not win over the nations to monotheism, in its own name. Judaism, instead, remained the national faith of the Jewish people. Despite the fact that many Romans did convert to Judaism, it became clear that to be a Jew in the Roman Empire was a severe political liability. After all, Rome had brought Judea to its knees, destroyed its vaunted Temple in Jerusalem, and reduced Jews to the status of an enslaved nation. Could Romans be expected to accept as their own, the religion of a subject people—one, indeed, they themselves had defeated?

Nevertheless, despite this difficult psychological and political impasse, the Rabbis did not narrow their world-view or reduce their concern for universal man. In the realm of religious and ethical ideology they continued their daring and their creativity. In practical terms, however, they slowly withdrew from the "missionary race" with Christianity, and set about building a new religious and social structure for the Jewish people. They made possible the survival of Jews as a minority beyond the fall of the Temple, the loss of Zion, and through every other exile and dispersion, as "God's witnesses" to the end of time.

By making Christianity possible, Rabbinic Judaism saved biblical religion for the world. But it did not merely serve as a spiritual catalyst, without possessing a life and a future of its own. Everywhere one turns in contemporary Jewish life and thought, the genius of Rabbinic Judaism is still to be found. It assured its future through two novel religious institutions—the Rabbinate and the synagogue—and by its creation of a vast religious literature—*The Talmud.*

When the Torah and Prophets became a Book, the day of the prophets was over, but this was not the end of Judaism. Now that God's word was committed to writing, a new type of religious leader comes to the fore, neither a prophet nor a priest. First known as Scribe, later as Rabbi (Hebrew for "scholar-teacher"), he was seriously challenged and rebuffed by the priests, despite the fact that he never laid claim to their biblical prerogatives. When Jerusalem fell in the year 70 of the Christian era, the day of the Temple and the priests was over, too, nor was this the end of Judaism. Now, the Rabbi becomes the authoritative and unchallenged heir of both prophet and priest. Now, too, the synagogue emerges as a new and uniquely-Rabbinic religious center—a school and a sanctuary. The Rabbis did not create the synagogue, but it was they who shaped and adapted it as a major vehicle for their ethical universalism and their faith in Israel's future.

An examination of how the Rabbi and the synagogue came upon the scene and interacted with each other will prove useful in shedding light on the creative adaptiveness of Rabbinic Judaism, which inheres in the Jewish religion to this day.

The Synagogue and the Rabbi

When modern Jews refer to their synagogues as temples they are in error, from the point of view of history. There was only one Temple in Jewish life, the Jerusalem Temple on Mount Zion. That Temple, first built by Solomon, but destroyed by the Babylonian Nebuchadnezzar in 586 B.C., then rebuilt as the Second Temple, only to be destroyed by the Romans in the year 70 of the Christian era, had a biblical mandate. How it came to be built, maintained and operated was fully described in the Bible. A full set of laws and practices was minutely formulated to govern the institution of the Temple, the plan and purpose of which were divinely preconceived. Each day, morning and afternoon, there were sacrifices on the altar. Pilgrims from all over the land thronged to it—particularly during the three harvest festivals of spring, summer and fall. The building itself was elaborately and splendidly built, and its physical majesty was matched by the rich aura of the religious service conducted by the priests and the levitical choirs and orchestra, whose tones overflowed into the chambers and the outer courts.

The synagogue, in contrast, had a much humbler origin. It came upon the scene as a human accommodation to the circumstances of Jewish history sometime after the first Temple had been destroyed. Ironically, however, the exile of the Jews to Babylon—a negative factor—was responsible for establishing the need for a "portable" Jewish sanctuary, which ultimately became the synagogue. Since neither altar nor priest was allowed to function outside the central sanctuary in Jeru-

salem, the exiles sought to bind themselves together in
religious devotions that would tie them, at least senti-
mentally, to the Temple, its services and religious practices. We can picture them gathering in their homes on
the sacred day of the week, the Sabbath, to read to one
another from those sacred writings that may already
have been committed to parchment. After reading these
texts someone might lead in prayer, perhaps using the
very psalms that had been incorporated into the Temple service. Still others might interpret portions of these
sacred texts, relying upon the oral traditions that customarily were handed down from father to son.

Out of such new needs and conditions the synagogue
arose. From the very start, it centered in the congregation rather than in a sacred shrine or a magnificent
building. Even when the exiles returned to their land to
build the Second Temple they carried attachments to
this new and popular form of religious expression.
From this time forward, despite the existence of the
Temple, emphasis begins to shift, although almost im-
perceptibly at first, from the sanctity of the *priests* to
the *people* themselves; from the place of worship, to
the gathering of worshippers—the people as a *holy
congregation.* This is the *edah,* which the Rabbis came
to sanction as a formal religious congregation of ten or
more males. Wherever they assembled—in private
homes, at the gates of the city, in the open fields—it
was *their religious motivations* as a congregation, not
the sacramental leadership of the priests, the sacred
ritual of the Temple, its sacrificial altar or sanctified
vessels, which came to dominate Jewish thought.

This new spirit was catching and synagogues sprout-
ed all over the land without plan or design, without an
established hereditary or hierarchical clergy. Indeed,
far from becoming a rival to the Temple as an institu-

tion of protest and rebellion, the synagogue was conservative and preservative. Thus, its prayer services
were modeled after the Temple service and were recited twice daily, mornings and evenings, at the very
hours of the sacrificial offerings in the Temple. Later,
after the Temple's destruction in the year 70, the synagogue liturgy was broadened and even made to include
the recitation of daily prayers for its speedy restoration,
"quickly, in our time, O Lord." And as a perennial reminder of the supreme sanctity of the Temple, the
"orientation" of the synagogue meeting-place was, and
is, toward Mount Zion in Jerusalem. Officially, the
synagogue awaited the day when the Temple would be
rebuilt. Yet, even when Solomon's Temple was replaced by the building of a Second Temple, after Ezra's
return from the Babylonian captivity, the synagogue
did not disappear. In Jerusalem alone, the very city of
the Temple, four or five hundred synagogues were said
to exist, and something new was now added to the
Temple itself: a chapel for prayer!

While the synagogue substituted prayer for Temple
sacrifice—thus, it had no altar—it became even more
than a "House of Prayer." Under the influence of the
Rabbis it was made into a "House of Study," a popular
school of higher spiritual learning for *adults*. The reading and teaching of Scripture became a central, characteristic feature of Jewish public worship, and a lecture
or homily given by recognized scholars was a regular
instructional device which had been built into the service. Learning God's will, by studying the Torah,
Prophets—and now, their Rabbinic interpretations, too
—was made into an act of worship in the synagogue. To
this day, synagogues still continue to emulate their
older counterparts: even the smallest congregation will
rarely fail to have a library-study hall, known as

"House of Study," with a formidable library of books dealing with the ethics, theology, jurisprudence and philosophy of Judaism. Pictorial art was precluded from both Temple and synagogue by the commandment prohibiting graven images; not to emulate the Temple, the grandeur of its architecture or funishings was never lavished upon any synagogue; its old and rare books became the "art" of the synagogue. With its scholarly tomes and volumes, the *Beth Hamidrash* (literally: "House of Study"), or study hall, of each synagogue was considered to be its treasure center. Indeed, so central to the life of the synagogue is the idea of study and learning that, in the Yiddish language, a synagogue is actually called *shul* which, as its German source—*schule*—of course, means a "school."

In addition to the two functions of the synagogue already described—a "House of Prayer" and a "House of Study"—it also was regarded as a "House of Assembly." The synagogue building served as a public center where matters of public and communal concern could be aired. Courts of law met in its rooms, heard testimony, administered oaths, and proclaimed judgments. Strangers to the community were welcomed into its hostel, the poor were invited to receive alms there, and community philanthropies were administered by its councils. In time, these communal functions of the synagogue became so integrated with its religious and educational purposes that, by the Middle Ages, the practice had developed whereby one could interrupt the services in order to inform the entire community of wrongs and injustices not yet redressed. The strong emphasis the synagogue placed on these various human needs of the community rather than upon its physical setting was responsible for the fact that its architecture became a matter of relative indifference to the Jewish community. As a building it was almost nondescript: hardly distinguishable as a religious landmark, and, from country to country, an unexciting edifice reflecting the style of its time and place.

The synagogue was surely not the Temple, the central ecclesiastical stronghold radiating its majestic splendor far afield. But it became something the Temple never was: a community center for prayer, for study, and for ethical striving through the alleviation of human hurt. At the outset, a *temporary* substitute for the Temple, later a parallel to it, it never saw itself as the Temple's replacement, although it has long since exceeded and transcended it! The synagogue has become the dynamic response of the resilient Jewish spirit to a changing and challenging environment, a unique institution molded and directed—to this day—by the religious teachings of Rabbinic Judaism. It succeeded in universalizing Jewish religious teaching which, in the hands of the Temple priesthood, was losing its prophetic stamp, and was becoming identified with a national cult and a single, national religious center.

But without the emergence of the Rabbi and the development and ultimate establishment of the Rabbinate as the authoritative heir of prophet and priest, the synagogue would have been bereft of the religious rationale and ideology necessary for its universalism. Today, synagogues and Rabbis are institutionally united: Rabbis usually function as the spiritual leaders of specific congregations. But when Rabbis first appeared on the scene, as Scribes, the idea was not altogether popular. True the prophets were laymen—and they often opposed the priestly ways—but they were chosen by God, himself, and, in any case, prophecy seemed to have come to an end. Who, then could now serve as the legitimate successors to the prophets? Who would be the new teachers of Israel and the world?

The people held conflicting views to this key question and they divided in terms of their social and economic stations and their general philosophy of life. The various antagonists developed their attitudes and fostered their programs through parties, or fellowships. At the outset, the largest and most influential party was the Sadducees, so called because they were led by members of the Sadok family of high priests. Sadducee adherents came, of course, from the priestly sector of the population, but also from wealthy aristocrats whose conservative views had been shaped by the priestly tradition. They took the view that the Torah itself had spelled out the only answer: authority to the priests to serve as the comprehensive religious leaders was divinely ordained. Thus, they argued, the priests were not only the rightful dispensers of ritual and guardians of the cult, at Temple worship, but they were also appointed as the protectors of the sacred text, the trusted teachers and interpreters of its laws and commandments. Accordingly, no teaching that was not specifically recorded in the biblical text could be countenanced; interpretations that were not literal were to be regarded as heretical.

Webster defines "Pharisee" as a hypocrite, "Pharisaism" as religious hypocrisy, or narrow, prideful legalism. The "Pharisee," thus, is still subjectively seen only as an object—of scorn and derision—not objectively regarded as subject, with a positive value of his own. He seems doomed "by definition," forever to remain as defined by his opponents: the early Christian writers who saw in him a great obstacle to the winning over of the whole Jewish people to Christianity. Other religious groups have, of course, known similar ironic fate—"character assassination by definition." Jesuits, for example, need only consult the same dictionary to discover that the descriptions given them by their rivals and enemies, from within and without the Church, make Webster's "Jesuit" something no real Jesuit could accept or believe possible.

Long before Christianity, the Sadducees looked scornfully upon those who opposed them and derisively dubbed them *Perushim,* Hebrew for Pharisees. By this name, which meant "separatists," the Sadducees wished to suggest that these Jews who questioned their priestly rule were, in fact, separating themselves from the people. The Pharisees, who were recruited principally from the lower social and economic classes, of course readily admitted that the Torah accorded the priestly families and Levites special prerogatives in the laws of purity and sacrifice. Indeed, the Pharisees agreed, the priests were set aside as a consecrated class to administer the ritual of the Temple. But the Torah had not granted them any other religious authority, the Pharisees argued. And as for the Sadducean claims concerning the written Torah (The Pentateuch) which they insisted had been entrusted to priests alone, the Pharisees countered with the concept of tradition. They contended that this tradition, which they called the oral Torah, went back to Sinai itself. There, God's word, the written Torah and its oral tradition were both given by Moses *to the whole people,* and not to the priests alone. The oral law is transmitted from generation to generation, and grows as interpretations in the light of new problems and conditions are added to it. No, the Pharisees rejoined, the tradition is not only a priestly one, congealed in words that are fixed and unyielding! It is a tradition given to the whole people, and those who will study and master it, may teach, expound and amplify it.

The Pharisee party had no official influence over the affairs of the community as long as the Sadducee priests were sovereign. Even after the Romans came to power, they were still regarded by the Emperor and his pro-consul as the "Establishment"—the recognized representatives of the Jews. Nevertheless, almost two centuries before Christianity, the Scribes were already gaining the confidence of the rank and file of the people; they soon came to be regarded as the backbone of the Pharisee party. The Pharisees would achieve importance once they could spread their influence throughout the country by means of the academies of learning they would establish. The curriculum of the *yeshiva,* or academy, centered in the elucidation of Scripture by applying the teachings of the oral law. In contradistinction to the rigid views of the priestly Sadducees, the students of the academies were exposed to varying interpretations of the law; each scholar customarily transmitted to his own disciples the traditions he had received from his own masters. In turn, the scholars of these academies handed down their own authority to their students to serve as masters of the law.

With the destruction of the Temple and the consequent waning of the priesthood, leadership began to move into the hands of those who could serve as judges. By reason of his knowledge of the law and his technical abilities as a student of Scripture, the Scribe now came to assume the power once held by the priest. After the destruction, the Scribe was called Rabbi, a title for what we might call the "diplomaed doctor of the law." The growth of the educated class as the teachers and expounders of the law became more and more pronounced, and they began to act as judges as

well as to expound. When, finally, the teacher also became the official judge, the importance of the priesthood was virtually diminished. The main question that
had plagued the community since the close of prophecy
had now been answered. Who indeed were the authentic successors of the prophets, the teachers and the
conscience of the Jewish community? The Rabbis, of
course! And who could be a Rabbi? Those who had
attended the academies and were authorized by their
scholar-teachers to be as one of them. The master laid
his hands upon his student, ordaining him as Rabbi. In
a public ceremony that was virtually the equivalent of a
modern diploma grant, the official transference of pedagogical authority from the master to pupil was made
known to all.

Even today, when modern Rabbis have become the
interpreters of Judaism through their personal leadership of specific congregations, rather than through their
attachment to the academies alone, they still retain
many of the characteristics of their ancient colleagues.
Like his first predecessors, the modern Rabbi is not a
priest, because he performs no ritual for his group—
only with it. But neither is the Rabbi a minister, because he never acts as God's authorized agent in offering access to personal salvation. This is why we have
called him a layman. And this is why, both in theory
and in fact, his ritual functions at Jewish services have
never been of any greater significance than those of the
humblest member of the congregation. Since he does
not administer sacraments or perform sacred rituals, he
is obviously but one of the members of the congregation, not a representative of divinity.

What, then, are the ritual and religious functions of
the Rabbi? It is the Rabbi, of course, who preaches the
sermon, on those occasions when sermons are given, on

Sabbaths and holidays. And this has remained the key to his role, from the days of Rabbinic Judaism until today. "Rabbi," we will recall, is the Hebrew name for "teacher." His preaching is essentially teaching, for his function remains to interpret the age in the light of the laws, traditions, and concepts of Judaism. Nor is his teaching task restricted to the pulpit. He is a "teaching elder" whose task it is to help infuse into the life of his congregation and others, an understanding of Jewish law and ethical tradition as they affect their whole life, every day of the week, everywhere they go.

But is he also a "ruling elder"?

Synagogue congregations are administered by boards of trustees who are duly elected according to the specific constitutional bylaws which each congregation freely enacts on its own. These men are responsible to the general membership in all matters relating to the finances and program of the congregation. The Rabbi is generally a member of the board of management, and his advice and counsel are often sought. However, he holds no veto power. Congregations are free to elect their own Rabbi for any length of time which is mutually desired, and Rabbis are under no compulsion to serve in a particular community for any specific period of time. This principle of voluntarism undergirds the relationship of Rabbi and synagogue in all areas, even in religious decisions. Since there is no central hierarchy in the Rabbinate, individual Jews are free to accept or to reject the interpretations of the law made by any particular Rabbi, or groups of Rabbis. But this does not mean that the Rabbi is without authority or influence. The authority of the Rabbi is primarily an "authority of influence" rather than an "authority of coercion." He exercises leadership by virtue of his scholarship, learning and moral virtue, rather than by any legal or divine right.

To be sure, some would say that "voluntarism" can lead to overindulgent autonomy, which, stretched to extremes, can result in chaotic, anarchical religious conditions. For this reason, there have been suggestions that the Rabbinate reestablish for modern times a counterpart of the ancient *Sanhedrin*, which, after the fall of the Second Temple, was taken over from the priests by the Pharisee Rabbis, and made into a central legislative body of 71 recognized scholars. On the other hand, other Jews find such an idea unwelcome. They regard the legitimacy of religious pluralism and diversity within Judaism as a highly-prized, hard-won contribution of Rabbinic Judaism to religious thought in general, and, moreover, as an important aspect of its creative genius. Indeed, the *Sanhedrin* which the Rabbis inherited from the Sadducean priests did become a recognized national forum, and the old priestly authority was centralized in the hands of the Rabbis at the top. Yet, despite this, the *Sanhedrin* of the Rabbis could never impose complete religious uniformity—the free and independent spirit of Pharisaism was too strong to allow that to happen. In Roman times, throughout Palestine—or later, in Babylonia, and later still, in medieval North Africa and Europe—the local Rabbinical Academy, the *yeshiva,* was more than a school. It was, in effect, a school of thought: differences of biblical interpretation and divergent religious practices thus became the accepted pattern of Jewish life which had been fostered by Rabbinic Judaism. The spirit of the oral law—a flexible, growing tradition—continued to be felt, even after these oral teachings of the Rabbis were codified as *The Talmud.*

Talmudic Literature

The Talmud, not a book but a vast literature, the collective work of many generations of Rabbis, serves as the essential testament of Rabbinic Judaism. It comprises more than 6,000 folio pages, the contents of which were formed over a period of almost 1,000 years —from almost two hundred years before to about five hundred years after the beginning of the Christian era. There are references in *The Talmud* to more than 2,000 scholar-teachers who participated in its deliberations—Rabbis who lived in Palestine or Babylonia.

At first, the oral teachings and unwritten traditions that each generation handed down to the next, were not permitted to be committed to writing. Perhaps this custom was adopted in order to prevent any other book or books from rivalling the Bible, the written law, in importance. But with the passage of time, and the growth of Talmudic thought, it became impossible for any one man to master the whole body of oral teaching. Sometime about the year 200 of the Christian era, *The Mishna* (meaning "Teaching"), a major compilation of the oral law, was codified and edited, in Palestine by the leading scholar of that day, Rabbi Judah. While most Jews of that time no longer used Hebrew in daily speech, but spoke a sister Semitic tongue, Aramaic, *The Mishna* was written in Hebrew, to maintain an unbroken line with the biblical past.

Together with the Pentateuch, *The Mishna* became the basic religious text of the Rabbinical academies in Palestine and Babylonia. Then, in Babylonia, about the year 500, a second Rabbinic code was edited. This was called *The Gemara* (which, in Aramaic, also means "teaching") and it was a compilation of the various discussions and religious developments which had taken place in the academies since the time of the appearance of *The Mishna,* some 100 years earlier. *The Gemara* was compiled in two editions, one in Palestine, the other in Babylonia, the Babylonian being the more significant of the two. The Babylonian *Gemara* was then added to *The Mishna* to make up *The Talmud,* which became the basic document of Rabbinic Judaism since it reflects the growth and development of Jewish law and thought over so many years. Since then, subsequent generations of Jewish scholars have made *The Talmud* into a subject of continuous inquiry and reverent reinterpretation and have written numerous commentaries and treatises based upon its teachings. Indeed, before a man is ordained as Rabbi, he is examined by his teachers in *The Talmud,* and is expected to be conversant with this basic source, so that his own decisions can be authentically rendered in the light of Rabbinic tradition.

What are some of the salient features of that tradition?

Someone has said that if religion is anything, it is everything. For the Rabbis, the Bible was everything—the source of life and understanding—since it was God's word to man. They took the Bible seriously as divine revelation and sought to find in its every word, nuances that would apply to the evolving human situation in its day-to-day experience. While they did not regard themselves as prophets, they did align themselves with the humane prophetic views over against the ritualistic disciplines and literalistic interpretations of the priests.

The prophets had spoken of immorality in high places, of the need to love the oppressed, and to build the just society. The Rabbis incorporated this warm and loving feeling for humanity into the daily habit of every Jew by means of the *Halaka,* which literally means "walking." *Halaka* is the walking in the "way of the Lord." Its critics, from the outside, often described Rabbinic *halaka* as arid legalism, the pouring of religious content into the small bottles of petty, ritualistic Rabbinic *halaka* as arid legalism, the pouring of religious revolution wrought by the Rabbis knows how far from the truth such a description is. The Pharisee-Rabbis were ranged against the Sadducee-priests. What the priests had made into the cold and impersonal commands of Scripture, Rabbinic *halaka* clothed with the warmth of a new zeal: to build God's kingdom on earth by learning to do his will within the human situation. This meant that all 613 commandments of Scripture had to be carefully and lovingly restudied, from the point of view of human need. In the priestly tradition the commandments were regarded as means of *sanctifying God. Halaka* made more of the commandments: they now were required to yield opportunities for the sanctification of human life. The *halaka* of the Rabbis reshaped prophetism and gave its lofty, humane concerns a concrete order and structure. Every commonplace, daily human habit could become sacred if it were seen—as the Rabbis insisted it should be seen—as an act of worship. The loving deed became more important than the cult of the Temple.

The Rabbis proceeded apace to build new rituals, "rituals of interpersonal behavior." The commandments of the written Torah—the Pentateuch—had been very specific and detailed when it came to rules relating to the sacrificial laws and priestly regulations. But what precisely did it mean when it said: "Honor thy father and thy mother"; or "Love thy neighbor as thyself"; or, "Remember that you were once slaves in the land of Egypt"? The Rabbis deliberately concerned themselves with such questions, and the answers they gave made their oral Torah into much more than a commentary or tradition. They deepened, humanized and universalized it. As the priests had been concerned with codifying the rituals of the cult, the Rabbis sought to codify love, loyalty and human compassion, to transform these into inescapable religious duties of every Jew. How must one love his neighbor? What are the ways in which one must honor his parents? What must a man *actually* do to demonstrate to himself and others that he will not go back to slavery, but seek to remain free?

They answered such questions as these by giving the Pentateuchal commandments new meanings. What had been stated before as general propositions, they now spelled out as specific religious duties, incumbent upon all. In effect, they rebuilt the Jewish religion by translating what had been prophetic sentiment into a personal religion built on "propositions-in-action." Hospitality to wayfarers, visiting the sick, dowering the indigent bride, giving charity anonymously, attending the dead to the grave, and helping to bring peace to those who lack it: these duties, for example, were never actually adumbrated in the Bible, although they are generally felt in spirit. The Rabbis made them, and many like them, into new commandments, or *mitzvot,* and thus made communion with God an act that could and should be experienced everywhere and any time, with or without the Temple, the priests, or the sacrificial altar.

This strong emphasis which Rabbinic Judaism placed upon the individual gave new meaning to personal ethics, highlighted the role of prayer over against sacrifice and gave each person in Israel a priestly function. It was this preoccupation with the person, and not only with the group, that brought about the development by the Rabbis of a new religious doctrine: divine retribution in a future world. The Sadducees were opposed to this view because, they claimed, it was un-biblical, not specifically recorded in the written Torah. But the Pharisees were trying to solve the vexing problems of individuals: why do the righteous suffer and the wicked prosper? They therefore took over the teaching of the Prophets concerning the End of Days—a teaching about the redemption that was to come to Israel and the world—and *applied it to the life and death of the individual person.* In Biblical Judaism, death was a shadowy affair. The souls of the dead went to a nether world, which somehow was outside the realm of God's justice. Rabbinic Judaism changed this: the Pharisees taught that the body dies but the soul is immortal. God's justice, they thus made clear, extends beyond life —the souls of the righteous are with God, as the reward for their good deeds in life. Each individual soul receives its own just deserts. The Jew who has lived with God's commandments will be rewarded with future bliss, even though he may now suffer; he who has cast God's word aside, may temporarily prosper while alive, but he will surely be requited in the "world to come."

Out of concern for the individual and the meaning of his life, the Rabbis created this idea of "other-world-liness." Yet they never allowed the Jews to neglect "this-worldliness." This is why the Talmud is extremely reticent and vague about the nature of the "world to come." The Rabbis continually cautioned their people against becoming overly-obsessed with this question. *The Mishna* specifically warns: "Whosoever gives his mind to what is above and what is beneath and what was before time and what will be hereafter, was better not to have been born!" Mystical longings for personal communion with God, passionate, pious hopes for the end of history and the immediate coming of a Kingdom not of this world, animated some Pharisees. These split off from the majority and left Jerusalem for the desert, to establish their own religious communities. We have long known about some of them from the ancient writings of the Jewish historian, Josephus. He describes one group of break-away Pharisees, the Essenes, depicting their communal life in the desert as they wait for the destruction of Rome and the beginning of the End of Days—of the world to come—now! Others, we have only recently learned about: these are the Dead Sea sects whose religious life has been unearthed with the discovery of the so-called Dead Sea Scrolls. They, too, had broken off from the Pharisees, and concentrated their prayers and hopes on the Kingdom of God, which they felt was at hand.

But the major emphasis of the Pharisees was away from such preoccupation with the world to come and mystical efforts to help bring it about. "The hidden things," they repeatedly warned, "belong to God." Man's primary tasks are here and now; God's Kingdom is here and now. In a fairly remarkable piece of biblical exegesis, a Talmudic Rabbi resoundingly summed up the Pharisaic view of the best way to know God: "In the book of Jeremiah it is written: For thus saith the Lord of Hosts, the God of Israel. 'Me have they forsaken and they have not kept my law.' This is what God is really saying: 'Would that men forsook me, if only they kept my law.'" Clearly, the Rabbis believed that the way to God was not through mystical retreat from day-to-day reality and responsibility, not by spending one's religious energies in seeking to understand the nature of God, but rather the Kingdom of God is built by those who accept the yoke of his commandments, now!

This is the way they resolved the question of reward and punishment for the future—without giving up the present, without over-speculating about the future. Those Jews who sought to gain life eternal could do so only by living out, now, all of the commandments of the Lord. These commandments, or *mitzvot,* as they are known in Hebrew, have been regarded by some as merely legalistic and ritualistic demands of a law that could not bring the Jew near, but only keep him far from God. Nothing could have been farther from the minds of the Rabbis. In their hands, the *mitzvot* became part of a religious system which was geared to a single purpose: regular and daily encounters with God. If their people were to remain "a holy nation" then, they believed, it had to be attached to a way of life that afforded repeated encounters with the holy that it might preserve an undiminishing awareness of God's glory. Without the experiences of awe provided by encounters with the divine, life's mystery is missed, and the extraordinary becomes commonplace.

Thus, the Rabbis built into this system of *mitzvot* a series of daily benedictions wherein the "King of the Universe" was intimately known and addressed by even the humblest member of the community as "Thou." Every time food was taken, or the rainbow seen, wisdom taught, or beauty experienced, the Jew was enjoined to pause in the midst of his preoccupation and personally to address the Lord, Creator of all things. When, for example, he partakes of food, he recites: "Praised be *Thou,* O Lord *our* God, King of the *Universe,* who bringest forth bread from the earth." Three ideas of God are experienced and known in this benediction, as in every other daily benediction the Rabbis required: First, the God who is praised is *my* God, for I speak to him, in intimate, personal address—directly, regularly, and without mediation. Second, the God who is addressed is *our* God, the one God known by the Jewish people, who were "discovered" by him, and who have maintained a very special relationship to him ever since. Third, this God—who merits "my" praise and deserves "our" gratitude—is "King of the Universe," the God of the whole world, Creator of heaven and earth.

In such ways as these, the Rabbis made clear to their people that the remote, transcendent God is at the very same time near, and that he holds together the destiny of the world, of this people, and of each individual. God is the Creator, and though man is dependent upon him as a creature, he is not lost in some whirring cosmos, but intimately related to him. God is the God of Israel, but he is also the Lord of creation and of history, and he is worthy of the worship of all men.

But what of these others, the non-Jews? How did they achieve salvation in the "world to come?" Did they, too, have to follow the commandments? Did they have to convert to Judaism in order to benefit from the blessings of the Torah?

The answers given to questions such as these by the Pharisee-Rabbis provide important insight into the universalism of Rabbinic Judaism. We have already discussed the drive toward proselytization that motivated the thinking of the early Rabbis, before Rome became so tremendously powerful. To be sure, they had ardently wished to bestow the benefits of the Torah and its commandments upon all nations. But failing this, they still made room for the "righteous non-Jew" in God's world to come. As his covenant-people, God had given Israel the Torah and they were required to keep all 613 of its commandments. Of the "Sons of Noah"—as the Rabbis called the non-Jews—God would only require that they keep seven commandments. "The Seven Commandments of the Sons of Noah," as defined by the Talmud, consist of six prohibitions: idolatry, improper use of God's name, murder, sexual immorality, theft, and inhumane conduct, such as the eating of the flesh of a living animal. In addition there was laid down the positive injunction requiring that courts of law and a system of justice be established. Those men and nations, the Rabbis contended, who lived faithfully by these Seven Commandments, were seen by God as if they had fulfilled the whole Torah. They had "a share in the world to come," as righteous men.

Indeed, the greatest Talmudist of the Middle Ages, Maimonides, based his authoritative teaching of Judaism's relation to Christianity and Islam on this Talmudic doctrine of the earlier Rabbis. Long before modern ecumenism was thought about, in 12th-century Moorish Spain, this Rabbi-Physician laid down the view: "The teachings of the Nazarene and of the Ishmaelite (Mohammed) serve the divine purpose of preparing the way for the Messiah, who is sent to make the whole world perfect by worshipping God with one spirit; for they have spread the words of Scriptures and the law of truth over the wide globe, and whatever of errors they adhere to they will turn toward the full truth at the arrival of the messianic time."

The Rabbis were devoted to making the life of each individual Jew a reflection of his personal priesthood as a member of a holy people which was to be a light unto the nations. Nevertheless, they taught their people to regard other "righteous men," and particularly those who shared their monotheism, as partners, not as rivals. The Talmudic literature they created made possible the accommodation of Judaism to the world they had to face—a world of exile and dispersion. But it did more: it preserved them intact in the midst of many nations, and made them ready to face the modern age.

IV

Modern Judaism

Modern Judaism, the religious life of Jews in the contemporary age, has roots in Rabbinic Judaism, and both go back to Biblical Judaism. But it is more directly the product of the modern temper that began to descend upon the Jewish community at the beginning of the 19th century. In the western world, Modern Judaism is expressed in the three religious movements—Orthodox, Conservative and Reform—which have emerged over the past century or so. Before attempting to evaluate the views which have set them apart, it is useful to trace the historical factors that helped to bring them into being.

As we have seen, the Talmudic Rabbis in the Diaspora of Babylonia had established patterns of living that encompassed the entire life-situation of the Jews, and these operated in ways that would make possible the survival of this people as a culture within a culture. In the 7th century, many Jews left Babylonia for North Africa and Spain. Jewish life continued to flourish under Islam, and the Near Eastern and Mediterranean Jewish communities together with their fellow Sephardi Jews in Spain (*Sepharad* means "Spain" in Hebrew) produced a unique intellectual culture in which scientific investigation—spurred by their intimacy with

Moslem culture—grew at the side of mysticism, theology, philosophy, and poetry. In that relatively "open society," it was possible for Jews to experience a "Golden Age" of creative cultural growth, until the days of the Inquisition in Christian Spain, and their expulsion in 1492.

The Ashkenazi Jews (*Ashkenaz* means "Germany" in Hebrew) had been living meanwhile in western Europe under Christian rule, and their life was one of relative isolation from their neighbors. While the Sephardi Jews were basking in the sun of Moorish culture for almost 600 years, the Ashkenazis were living in Europe's "Dark Ages." Their development took a different turn. Cast out from the world of Christianity, they made their domain the world of the Torah and the Talmud. Their law, science, art and philosophy were all part of one fabric: the word of God as revealed to their ancestors at Sinai. The scholars, of course, wrote in Hebrew, the "Holy Tongue." But some time during the Middle Ages the mass of Ashkenazi Jews absorbed the medieval German language and made it their own, by liberal additions of Hebrew words. This Judeo-German language came to be known as Yiddish, and from those years until only very recent decades, this was the universal language spoken all over the world by Ashkenazi Jews.

Medieval Jewry was subjected to one terror after another. Forced to move about from land to land, the one stable factor of its life was the *halaka,* which bound Jew to Jew, and all together, wherever they might go, to God. As a nation within nations—Jews had no civil rights, no permission to own land or join guilds—the synagogue served as the national center of their own "welfare state." Education, religion, charity, social welfare, indeed all their human needs, found their base in the synagogue. The law that governed their community life was the same law that was sovereign in their private habit: the oral and written Torah, which together constituted Rabbinic *halaka,* was their total way of life.

In response to the increasing terror inaugurated by the Crusades, the Ashkenazi Jews of western Europe began searching for new exiles. They traveled eastward, and by the 15th century had already established communities in Poland, and still later throughout most of eastern Europe. In Russia, they came upon old Jewish communities they knew nothing about, whose settlement went back to Byzantine days: brothers and sisters of those who had gone westward to North Africa and then Spain, a thousand years earlier. In Kiev, "mother of Russian cities," a community of Jews from the Middle East had settled even before the 8th century, thus antedating even the Russians. Ironically, eastern Europe, in the late Middle Ages, became the meeting ground of two separate streams of the Diaspora community: one which harked back to those who had come directly from the Near East through the Black Sea; the other, the newer refugees from western Europe, who now fled eastward. There, in eastern Europe, they were set apart from the Christian communities by the edict of one ruler after the other. In time, they established their own cohesive cultural structure which institutionalized Rabbinic Judaism as a force for Jewish unity throughout Europe.

The spirit of Enlightenment, which had begun to rise in Europe as early as the days of the Renaissance, did not descend upon the Jewish community until much later. It was in western Europe that it was first felt by Jews, but not until about the beginning of the 19th century. By then, some Jews in the West were located in the rising middle class. They not only spoke the same languages as their middle-class neighbors, but slowly began to adopt the same mentality and outlook. Rising now on the European horizon was a feeling of nationalism that was linked to the expansion of science, trade and industry. These changed economic and political conditions in the West, and opened up the Jewish community to the world around. Instead of maintaining a defensive posture, many western Rabbis were now willing to build intellectual bridges spanning Jewish religious thought and the new knowledge spawned by scientific inquiry. The mid-19th century in western Europe saw the beginnings of efforts to reform Judaism in terms of the new philosophies of the day, and in keeping with the spirit of scientific investigation.

In eastern Eruope, the situation of the Jews was totally different. The spirit of Enlightenment did not come to Jews in the Russian Empire until the second half of the 19th century. In the West, the Rabbis had accommodated to western culture, and had sought to reform traditional Judaism so that it could be recognized as part of the accepted western landscape. In eastern Europe, there was no possibility of transforming the Jewish community into a normal, respected sector of the Russian world; medieval attitudes still dominated the Russian outlook, and Jews were still officially set apart in ghetto-communities. But while no reformation of Judaism was thus possible in Russia, different phenomenon of the modern world did spread among these eastern-European Jews. This was the romantic expression of nationalism, and it took root among them in the form of political Zionism. This movement based itself on the modern concept of nationality: since Jews formed a separate nationality (at least in eastern Europe) they had the right to political normalcy, and they could achieve normalcy only if they because a nationality like all others, with a publicly recognized territory or state of their own.

The unique relationship of the land of Israel to the religion of Israel is a constant element in Jewish history. The Promised Land was more than a national goal, more than a vehicle of God's covenant with Israel. The Holy Land became the very stage for a system of biblical laws—agricultural and labor legislation—that gave meaning and focus to the ethical character of Judaism. Rooted in the very soil of the land of Israel are biblical laws dealing with social justice, the prevention of poverty, and the public concern due the orphan, the widow, and the dispossessed. Long after the Jews were exiled and forcibly separated from Palestine, and to this very day, the prayers of the synagogue continue to echo the people's nostalgia for the soil and the skies, the rain and the dew, the fruit and the trees of their ancestral homeland—the land of Israel.

Zionism borrowed its political theories from the modern world, but its attachments to Palestine as a national homeland stemmed from these older and deeper sources which flowed out of the religious teachings of Biblical and Rabbinic Judaism. Long years before the dawn of the modern political concept of nationality, pious Jews from various parts of the world continued to return to the Holy Land. There, at the end of their days, they would have the privilege of burial in the sacred earth of the Holy Land, in anticipation of their resurrection, which, they believed, would follow the arrival of messianic days. Indeed, the establishment in 1948 of the State of Israel has been regarded by many as infinitely more than a political achievement that afforded Jews a physical haven from their wanderings and persecutions. Many religious Jews see in it the hand of God, and the beginning of a new development in the history of the Covenant.

The State of Israel

For Christians, however, the emergence of a sovereign, independent Israel has brought into sharp focus the almost total theological unpreparedness for this new turn in Jewish history. For many Christians, Jewish peoplehood did not even seem to exist after the Roman exile and the Temple's destruction. Moreover, the dispersion of the Jews was regarded by many as a merited punishment of their rejection of Christianity. Wandering, dispersion, and exile—all of these were seen as normative for a people which had brought forth, but then rejected, the Savior. Clearly, the restoration of a representative portion of the people of Israel to its land, as a sovereign state recognized by the international community, was bound to raise many theological problems for Christianity.

In reaction, some Christians have been tempted to regard the State of Israel as only a secular phenomenon, outside the scope of the promises made by God to Israel. Others have suggested that Israel is a political matter and thus has no place in a Christian's religious approach to the Jewish people.

But sensitive Christians are becoming more and more aware that it is necessary to see the State of Israel as Jews see it, and not as others would like Jews to see it. Krister Stendahl, a leading Protestant, and the Dean of Harvard Divinity School puts the matter this way: "Israel's constitution guarantees freedom of religion, and retains the religious courts for Christians and Muslims in matters of marriage, etc. according to the ancient system inherited from the Turks and the British. But Israel is a

Jewish State and its religion is Judaism. The driving forces which made Palestine—rather than Uganda—the goal for Zionism are reason enough for the intertwining of Jewish faith and the State of Israel. That force was rooted in the Scriptures and the tradition. Whether we like it or not when we speak and think about the State of Israel, we are speaking about a very substantial element of Judaism. Not only in terms of so many Jews, but also in terms of Jews who see the State of Israel as the fulfillment of God's promises."

Indeed, many Christians who were moving closer toward a dialogue with Jews on Judaism have come to sense what Father Edward H. Flannery, Executive Secretary of the American Bishops' Secretariat for Catholic-Jewish Relations, has suggested: "The large majority of Jews have identified with Israel. Most, in varying ways, see it as the greatest development in Jewish life covering hundreds, even thousands, of years. Whether they see it as an answer to the problem of anti-Semitism, a source of Jewish identity, or as a messianic fulfillment, they see it, in any case, as central to their Judaism or Jewishness and insist that it be discussed in the dialogue. Dialogue is a conversation between two parties, and one of the first rules of dialogue is that each party be allowed to enter it on the basis of self-definition. If Jews assure Christians that Israel is an integral part of their Judaism and that it should be on the agenda of the dialogue, Christians should accept this. It is time Christians commenced asking Jews, instead of Christians, what Judaism is."

What then do Jews ask of Christians in this regard? Again, reflecting the view of those Christians who regard the renewal of the Jewish people as a vital spiritual necessity for the world, Father Flannery makes these points:

"The fundamental issue in the Middle East, as Jews generally see it, and as I do myself, is the right of Israel to exist and develop in peace. This right has been threatened, by force in the past, and by proclamation of intent in the present . . . We must affirm Israel's right to stay securely on the soil which her farmers, workers, thinkers, and teachers have reclaimed by the sweat of their brows. As Christians, we must go even further: The people of Israel not only have a right to live—they have a vocation to live for the Lord. We hope that it will be granted them to bear witness to the God of Abraham, Isaac, and Jacob on His favored land, as never before . . . It is especially the Christian who is expected to rejoice at the upturn in the fortune of Jews that Zionism, or any other agency, has brought about in our time."

Reform Judaism

The Reform movement in Judaism began in the middle of the 19th century, chiefly in Germany and America, as a radical answer to the new discoveries in science, history, and comparative religion. It broke with tradition in its attitude to *halaka,* and denied the binding authority of the Bible and the Talmud on questions of ceremonial and ritual law. Reformers replaced Hebrew, the basic language of prayer, with the vernacular, as a symbol of their common bond with fellow citizens of other faiths. Dietary laws and other rituals which smacked of social segregation or seemed too oriental for the western mind were omitted from the religious regimen. At the synagogue service, the organ was introduced to "modernize" and enhance the ritual, and the family pew, for men and women, took the place of the traditional segregation of the sexes at worship. Supernatural authority was denied as the basis for the ceremonial law contained in the Bible and the Talmud. The greatest stress was placed upon the ethical teachings of the Prophets, and the mission and vocation they had given Israel as the bearer of "ethical monotheism" to the world were placed at the center of Reform theological interest.

For many years, the Reform congregations were extremely individualistic and characterized by a desire to experiment radically in every sphere of religious practice. For a time, some had cast out the Saturday Sabbath, hallowed by Jewish history and tradition, and were seriously thinking of introducing Sunday, the Christian Sabbath, in its place. Virtually all gave up the older belief in a Messiah as a physical redeemer, and cast out, as well, the idea of the restoration of Israel to Zion as a necessary precondition for the ultimate redemption. They did not accept a literalist view of revelation and preferred to be subjectively selective in what they often considered the human inspiration, not the divine revelation, of the Bible.

More recently, however, Reform Judaism has retraced its earliest steps, and while it still remains a liberal, experimentalist grouping, much that is traditional has been reintroduced into the thought-life of its congregations. The theological apartness between Reform and the more traditional religious sections in Modern Judaism has been steadily narrowing. Slowly, the humanist and naturalist God-views, which had been so dominant in Reform Judaism until recently, are being displaced by more traditional Jewish theological attitudes. The most significant differences that still remain have to do with ritual practices rather than with religious beliefs.

Orthodox Judaism

Rabbinic Judaism, we have seen, created a comprehensive community, capable of generating a spiritually and culturally autonomous Jewish life everywhere in the world. This is the style of life Orthodox Judaism still desires to preserve and to perpetuate, through devout religious loyalty.

Leaders of Jewish Orthodoxy prefer the name Traditional Judaism. They are convinced that what they call Judaism is, in fact, the traditional way Jews have lived since the days of the Talmud, and that other approaches are inauthentic and will lead to the assimilation of the Jewish people.

Orthodox Judaism regards both the written law of Moses and the oral law of the Rabbis as authoritative and binding, and it considers that every question facing man today can be answered in the light of these ancient, divine teachings. Thus, almost instinctively, the Orthodox Jew tends to meet every life-situation with what he calls a "Torah-true approach." What, he asks himself, must he do, if he is to respond as God would have him respond? He will consult with the learned, with Rabbis, for their understanding of the matter. Yet, since he is Orthodox, it is quite likely that he, himself, has been thoroughly immersed in religious studies, and will have developed an educated intuition into the answers that Orthdoxy would deem proper. When his questions are of profound difficulty, he will submit them to a Rabbi for adjudication and decision. Of all three religious groupings in Modern Judaism, Orthodoxy has the greatest regard for the Rabbi—one should say, the Orthodox Rabbi—as the recognized teacher and interpreter of the *halaka*.

Even within Orthodoxy, however, the authority of

the Rabbi is not everywhere the same. In North America, individual Orthodox Rabbis and synagogues are federated together in countrywide associations. Here, they have joined in voluntary ways for mutual counsel and advice, and none is required to submit to any outside authority. In some countries, like Great Britain, Orthodoxy is governed by the Office of a Chief Rabbi, whose decisions in religious questions all member-congregations and Rabbis have agreed to accept. In the State of Israel, where the Millet system of the Middle East obtains, religious officials—in this case, the Orthodox Rabbinate—are regarded as having an official governmental function, and thus, many of their decisions are binding upon the whole Jewish community—the non-Orthodox, as well.

While the Orthodox are unanimous in their belief in the literal revelation of the Torah and the need to submit to the teachings of Talmudic Judaism, there is no unanimity regarding interpretation of these laws. A rather wide range of opinion exists. Some, recognizing that *halaka* grew, metamorphosed and developed, are likely to urge that more serious attempts be undertaken to expand the *halaka,* to renew it, to adapt it to the world of the 20th century. Others, however, tend to recede from such views, fearing that a stretching of the tradition may, indeed, tear it asunder.

All groups within Orthodoxy agree, nevertheless, that the only valid way to treat Jewish law and tradition is by applying the due process of its principles and precedents to the living situation. And this can only be done by means of learning: it is incumbent upon every Jew to study and to observe, and without the former, the tradition says, there is little significance to the latter. This explains why Orthodoxy places such strong emphasis upon education, and why it is that despite the many sacrifices it entails, thousands of Orthodox Jewish parents send their children to religious schools where traditional learning can be acquired, in addition to general, secular studies. There is little doubt that Orthodoxy makes the greatest demands upon its adherents, demands that can even carry social or economic penalties. For example, it is not easy for Jews who work in non-Jewish environments to follow the Kosher food laws, or to refrain from labor on their Sabbaths and festivals. It is interesting, nevertheless, to note a resurgence of Orthodoxy today, after many years of decline. Yet, the strength of Orthodoxy is not related to numbers. It helps to remind all other Jews of the fullness of the tradition, even those who cannot always accept all of its teachings.

Conservative Judaism

The reformers of Judaism in the 19th century helped to create a renaissance in Jewish religious scholarship, in their effort to find support for their modern views. But dissatisfactions arose on the part of other Jewish scholars who felt that they had placed a one-sided emphasis on the universal elements in the Jewish past, without taking into account the uniquely Hebraic character of its spirit. As a result, there grew up in a number of European countries, and more especially in North America, a school of thought that spoke of the need to emphasize the "positive-historical" elements of the tradition. They prepared the way for what was to become known as the Conservative movement in Judaism. In contrast to Reform, the Conservatives emphasize the distinctive elements in Judaism, asserting that the need to *preserve* the Jewish people as the vehicle of the tradition in no way contradicts the universalism of Judaism. In contrast to

Orthodoxy, however, Conservative Judaism places high priority on the need to examine the *halaka,* and to change it wherever necessary, in accordance with its spirit, but based upon a desire to direct its growth. Acknowledging, as do the Orthodox, the revered place of the Bible and the Talmud, the Conservatives, however, are not committed to the principle of literalism in their interpretations. The law, they feel, must be both binding and susceptible of change.

For a long time, the leaders of Conservative Judaism viewed themselves as do the Orthodox—not as partisans of a sectarian Judaism, but as followers of authentic, traditional Jewish life. The earliest Conservatives in America felt that their method—tradition with change—was the very method adopted during the most creative periods of Rabbinic Judaism. The essential spirit of Rabbinic Judaism, they pointed out, was the adaptive talent, the capacity to make prophetic Judaism come alive in a unique way, within the personal life, or, through the method of reinterpretation to bring biblical teachings "up-to-date" by making them relevant to the life of succeeding generations. Changes, to meet the challenge of growth, were characteristic of the Rabbinic tradition, the Conservatives maintained. Accordingly, certain experiments were countenanced within individual congregations—experiments with the liturgy and with certain ritual practices. But many of these, like the introduction of *Bat Mitzvah* for girls (see below), the seating of men and women together at services, or the organ at synagogue worship, were considered by the Orthodox to be far removed from traditional Jewish experience. Inevitably, the Conservatives were to be regarded by the Orthodox not as traditional or authentic, but as a deviating, denominational grouping. Nor were the Orthodox seen any longer by the two other groups—

the Reform and Conservative—as the only legitimate expression of tradition.

As a religious movement of the center, Conservatism values much in Reform, to its left, and in Orthodoxy, to its right. It appreciates the emphasis of Reform on classical Jewish prophecy: the concern for social justice, for the spread of peace and love throughout the world. It also admires the tenacity of Orthodoxy in maintaining the warm traditional life, despite the many hardships this may entail. But it goes its own way, asserting with the medieval sage: *"God, Torah, and Israel are One."* This theological equation serves to underscore the emphasis Conservative Judaism places upon the interrelationship of the three components of the tradition: faith and trust in *God* as the source of life; living out God's will by knowing and keeping his word, which is in the *Torah;* the importance of the people of *Israel,* its life, its history and its future, as the covenant-people.

The Conservatives have felt that Reform Jews neglected the concepts of Torah and Israel, in concentrating their universalism on God alone. The Orthodox, they believed, had stressed God and Torah, but had neglected to be concerned with the living reality of Israel—the immediate religious and spiritual needs of the Jewish people, in this time and place.

The relationship between the people and the religion is unique in Judaism. Indeed, without a continuous, ongoing, living Jewish people, the religion of Israel is quite inconceivable. Judaism has assimilated individuals, even nations, into its ranks. But were the Jews to disappear as a group, inevitably Judaism would disappear with them. The indissoluble bond between the people and the religion has made it possible to define Judaism as "the evolving religious civilization of the Jewish people." True, the prophets of Israel have become universal religious figures. Yet, they themselves would have seen their vocation principally as the teachers of their own people whose sins and sorrows were the focal point of their spiritual broodings. Israel is more than a law, more than a creed: it is a people!

Thus, to be true to historical Judaism, the Conservatives have felt it necessary not only to be accountable to the demands of God and his Torah, but to be equally sensitive to the physical and spiritual needs of the Jewish people. Such views have made Conservative Judaism especially relevant to the North American Jews who have felt a strong need to retain their spiritual identity in lands that encourage religious pluralism. In these lands of freedom, there is always the danger of their spiritual isolation from the rest of Jewry throughout the world. The Conservative emphasis upon the *people of Israel,* as a unitary historical and spiritual entity, has made them alive to this reality and has given broad spiritual scope to their self-awareness as Jews.

All three groups hold more in common than their division seems to indicate. All stress belief in the unity of God and proclaim their joint desire to bear witness, as Jews, to the word of God, as given to their ancestors, at Sinai. All are in agreement with most of the traditional theological concepts, although each grouping gives these their own shadings and interpretations. It should be noted that all three names—Reform, Orthodox and Conservative—are borrowed from the world of Christian denominationalism, and are, in effect, adjectives that have come into vogue only in modern times. Modern Judaism, to be sure, like all of Gaul, is divided into three parts. Essentially, however, it is the noun "Judaism" that is more important to all three groups, than the new-found adjectives, "Reform," "Orthodox," or "Conservative."

The modern world has given birth to Modern Judaism —three versions of the same ancient teachings. Yet, no Jewish congregation may be rightfully challenged regarding its authority to speak in the name of the tradition. This is so because, to begin with, the synagogue is not considered to be the authoritative, divine instrument for dispensing salvation. To be sure, the Jewish tradition claims the "chosenness of Israel." But it never thinks of the synagogue as the means whereby chosenness is either conferred or assured. In Modern Judaism, as ever before, chosenness implies the responsibility which Jews have as a community or group, inside or outside the synagogue, to bear witness in their personal lives and in their communal association, to the oneness of God and of mankind. And the Jewish tradition—whether in its old forms or new versions—insists that this can come about, not through the ordinances of an ecclesiastical unit such as a synagogue, but *only* by the *personal* fulfillment of God's teachings—the *mitzvot*—on the part of the individual Jew as a member of the Jewish community.

With these views of Modern Judaism in mind, we are now ready to embark on a "spiritual tour" of Jewish worship and life, as presently experienced and actually practiced.

PART TWO

The Jewish Year: The Worship of the Lord

V

Inside the Synagogue

One of the very first distinguishing marks that greets the stranger upon entering an Orthodox or Conservative synagogue is the unusual sight of men worshipping with their heads covered, wearing hats or skullcaps. This is another custom that has come out of the East. It is a reminder, once again, that Judaism has its origin in the land of Palestine, and that, through all these years, it still bears many of the hallmarks of the East. For while we cannot very easily ascribe a single, simple reason as being responsible for this custom, which has become a hallowed tradition among Jews, we do know that it is in part due to the manners and customs of the eastern world. Western man raises his hat in respectful greeting, but the Near East is accustomed to doing just the opposite. For an oriental to appear bareheaded before his guests is a breach of good manners which would be deeply resented. This conventional gesture of politeness toward one's fellowmen eventually must have become a sign of awe and respect in the presence of God, and it took on all the aspects of a sacred custom. Moreover, the High Priest of old, when officiating in the Jerusalem Temple, was distinguished by a miter made of fine cloth, which was coiled around his head like a turban. A diadem of pure gold was fastened to it with a purple cord and it bore the inscription: "Holiness unto the Lord," a phrase summarizing the aim and the purpose of his office. When the Temple was destroyed, the office of the High Priest ceased to exist and thereafter the distinction between priesthood and laity became obsolete in Judaism. It is probable that the head-covering of the Jews at prayer has some relationship to this historical situation. Once the High Priest wore a miter on his head; now the people, having, so to speak, assumed the priestly role, wear miters as an act of symbolic remembrance.

Besides the head-covering, there is a second article of dress which is most striking to the stranger in the synagogue. This item, like the head-covering, is worn in Orthodox and Conservative but usually not in Reform congregations. It is called a *tallit,* or prayer shawl, and it is worn by adult males, although younger boys may often also wear it at services. The *tallit* resembles the style of an outer garment worn in ancient Palestine. In time, when Jews lived outside of Palestine and adopted other garments for dress, the *tallit* was set aside for ritual purposes alone. Its religious or ritual significance is especially related to fringes or *tzitzit* at each of its four corners. This is in accordance with the biblical prescription to "make . . . a fringe upon the corners of their garments . . . that you may look upon it and remember the commandments of the Lord." In early times these fringes were worn on the outer garments, and were a distinguishing mark of the Jews, who, even by means of their dress, desired to recall the commandments of God in the daily pursuit of life. Jesus, like his fellow Jews, wore fringes on his cloak, too. Indeed, in the episode of the woman with an issue of blood, the New Testament describes how she "came up behind him, and touched the fringe of his garment;

and immediately her flow of blood ceased" (Luke 8, 44). In later times because of their fear of persecution, Jews placed these fringes on a small undergarment, instead of wearing them on the outer garments. To this day, devout Jewish men wear this *Arba Kanfot,* or "four corners," as an undergarment, every day of their lives. The fringe, which is a symbol and a reminder of the commandments, was later adapted from this undergarment and placed upon the prayer shawl, which Jewish men wear at every morning service, whether at home or in the synagogue. Since the Rabbi and the cantor are essentially laymen and not priests, they, too, wear the same kind of prayer shawl at the synagogue service. In Conservative and Reform congregations, it has become the custom for those who lead the services to wear a black pulpit robe in addition to the cap and prayer shawl. In Orthodox congregations, usually only the cantor wears such a robe. But the robe is merely a matter of outer form and has no intrinsic religious significance.

In certain Protestant churches, the "Jewish prayer shawl" in the form of a clerical stole is worn by the officiating clergy during worship services. Roman Catholic priests wear six different sacred vestments in celebrating Mass—all of which are derived from ancient Jewish sources. Seeing a priest in this dress, one gets a better idea of what the officiants in the Jewish Temple of Jerusalem wore at their service. In the twenty-eighth chapter of the Book of Exodus, and the eighth chapter of the Book of Leviticus, detailed descriptions of the vestments of the priests of ancient Israel are given.

Music, as everyone knows, has been intimately associated, as have other arts, with the development of religion. The music one hears in the synagogue is based upon the cantillation of the Scripture and is different from the use of music in the ancient Temple. The Temple employed a priestly orchestra and Levitical choir. In the Book of Psalms, mention is made of the large number of instruments which were used in the Temple service. But the synagogue never emulated the Temple in this, as it had not in other ways, and so it frowned upon the use of instrumental music at its services. Indeed, after the destruction of the Temple, all instrumental music, even for religious purposes, was prohibited, as a sign of national mourning over the loss of the Temple. The synagogue *hazzan,* or cantor, was thus required to chant the liturgy without accompaniment, except for the congregational responses. Today, however, all Reform and a minority of Conservative congregations have introduced the organ into the music of the synagogue service.

The language, music and vestments of the synagogue still retain their own unique character. The music echoes with the cadences of the oriental background of Judaism: in the cantillations, one still hears the sounds which reverberated in the dwellings and marketplaces of ancient Near Eastern communities. The outward religious garb, the prayer shawl and head-covering are living vestiges of Semitic attire of the ancient Fertile Crescent.

Inside the synagogue, however modern its exterior architecture or its interior furnishing may be, these visible and audible signs of Jewish antiquity are a dramatic reminder of the survival of this people from earliest times.

VI

The Prayer Book

Siddur is the Hebrew word for prayer book, and it means "order." This reflects the highly liturgical and formal character of synagogue worship. Each day of the year, at least three services are recited—morning, afternoon and evening. The morning service may be recited any time after dawn until noon, the afternoon service from shortly after noon until dusk, and the evening service any time after sunset. For practical purposes, most synagogues arrange the daily morning service sometime before 9:00 a.m., to enable the worshippers to arrive at work at a reasonable hour. Similarly, the afternoon and evening services are usually said successively, just before the sun sets, and immediately following its setting, to facilitate matters.

The prayers for each service are clearly established and arranged in the prayer book, and from one synagogue to another (except Reform) there will be hardly any deviation. By and large, these services are conducted by the lay members of the congregation themselves, who act as their own cantors. On the yearly anniversary of a parent's death (*Yahrzeit*), it has become customary for sons to attend the three daily services, beginning with the evening before, and, in addition to reciting the *Kaddish,* to serve as the cantor, in reverent tribute to the memory of the deceased. As a result of this close relationship to both the conduct of the prayer services and the contents of the prayer book, the *Siddur* has become an intimately-known book to the devoted Jewish worshipper. Next to the Bible, the *Siddur,* which consists of many quotations from Scripture, is the most beloved text of the synagogue.

The single largest source for the prayer book is the Psalms, which covers a history of close to a thousand years, beginning as early as David (1000 B.C.) down to the time of the Second Temple. The Hebrew Psalter, consisting of 150 psalms, is often referred to as "the hymnbook of the Second Temple," because it was during the time that this Temple stood that the priests and Levites performed their rituals to the musical accompaniment of these inspiring and pious songs of divine praise.

The traditional Hebrew prayer book has a long and colorful history, containing elements that stretch over three thousand years. Obviously, then, it is not the work of one man but, like the Hebrew Bible, it is a reflection of the unfolding development of the Jewish people on its own land and in several diaspora communities.

It was not until the 9th century that the first complete *Siddur* was compiled and edited. Rabbi Amram, head of a major academy in Babylonia, and the foremost Jewish religious authority of the time, and his students, were jointly responsible for this. In addition to biblical material, they incorporated the prayers and benedictions which the Rabbis of the Talmud had written, and which had become part of the accepted traditional pattern. The structure of most services had been built around the *Shema* (Hear, O Israel . . .) and the *Amidah,* a prayer of silent devotion recited standing, containing nineteen Benedictions, erroneously called the "Eighteen," which contains but one prayer for personal prosperity and sustenance. The *Siddur* is exceptionally free from personal petition, for the Jewish language of prayer concentrates upon the plural, rather than the singular—the group, rather than the individual. Indeed, the Rabbis of the Talmud ordained that on the Sabbath and festivals it was improper to offer petitions to God which centered on private wants or needs —only the welfare of the group may be mentioned on those occasions.

The core of the *Siddur* is still the Psalter, and the "Book of Common Prayer" of the Anglican, Episcopal, and many Protestant Churches, not to mention the Roman Catholic Missal, was also shaped and influenced by the Psalms. (Indeed, the Rosary, while dedicated to Mary, is based upon Psalms, for the complete Rosary consists of 150 beads, divided into 15 sections of ten each—to correspond to the 150 Psalms of Hebrew Scripture.) Even the idiom of prayer in the Christian Church is often a direct borrowing from the Hebrew tradition:

The familiar and basic prayer, "Our Father" (*Pater Noster*), uses the plural form of petition—give *us,* forgive *us,* deliver *us*—just as it is done in the synagogue.

The idea of the "Kingdom of God" is a Hebrew phrase and concept, and comes into the Christian service straight out of the synagogue prayer book.

The "Lord's Prayer" is a shortened form of five of the original six of the "Eighteen Benedictions" found in the Hebrew prayer book, while the Sermon on the Mount is a terse summary of basic Pharisaic doctrine, and many of its ideas and phrases have been part of the synagogue service since the very beginning of its history.

The *Shema*—"Hear, O Israel, the Lord our God, the

Lord is One" (Deut. 6, 4)—is the central prayer of the synagogue, and the verses that immediately follow have been hallowed for centuries. The love of God with all one's heart, might, and soul, and the command to love one's neighbor as one's self (Lev. 19, 18)—which form an important and pivotal Christian prayer and teaching—are not only taken from the Hebrew Bible, but have also been echoed in the synagogue service for centuries.

The Hebrew language itself is still spoken at Church worship, and clergy and congregation often use words borrowed from the synagogue prayer book—words like *Hallelujah, Selah, Amen.*

Throughout their history, Jews have been multi-lingual. They have been forced into dispersion, and wherever the migrated they adjusted to the life and the language of the new lands into which they came. Although they spoke the language of their adopted countries, they nevertheless retained a knowledge of and an appreciation for their own language—Hebrew. In Orthodox or Conservative congregations, most of the religious service is still conducted in the Hebrew language, the national tongue of the Jewish people. The sermons, of course, are preached in English, and a number of English readings have been added to assist those members of the congregation who lack facility in reading or comprehending the Hebrew language.

If you should happen to attend one of the major services of the week, such as the Sabbath morning service, you will hear the cantor leading the liturgy in Hebrew melody. The reader, too, chants the weekly Scriptural lesson from the Torah Scroll (the Pentateuch) in the original Hebrew in much the same way that it was done in the synagogue, even before the time of Jesus. In the synagogue, hardly anything is read in a declamatory style, for the Hebrew prayers, many of which are from the Psalms and other poetical parts of Scripture, are all chanted. Even the worshippers chant the prayers aloud as they join in worship. But this should not be surprising if you remember that the chanting of prayers and the intoning of poems and sacred texts are very ancient customs which still survive in Judaism. Indeed, in this way each worshipper personally participates and is able to get the feeling and the rhythm of the words.

Prayer in the Hebrew language functions for Jews in much the same way that Latin does for Roman Catholics, but for different reasons. Hebrew is the national language of the Jewish people, and thus reflects its own historical civilization. No matter where Jews live, they are united to each other by the transcendental character of their own religious culture. It is not an accident of history that those Jewish communities which neglected the study of the Hebrew language led the way toward the total assimilation of Jews into the non-Jewish world, for the Hebrew language is infinitely more than a language of liturgy alone. Unlike Latin, it is not "dead" nor has it ever been dead. The language grew as life changed, for it was not merely the language of the synagogue, but the language of the people as well. In medieval times, additional works of great writings were created by the Jews. Poetry, philosophy, law and even science were fostered in Jewish communities from the shores of the western Mediterranean to the Persian Gulf. The Hebrew language developed apace, once again reflecting its inner vitality and growth. And in modern times as well, there has been a virtual renaissance of Hebrew language and literature which has found its center in the new State of Israel, and from there influences Jewish culture around the world.

But apart from cultural considerations, from a purely religious point of view, Hebrew remains a necessary tool for the Jew. Since the congregation participates in the religious service to a great extent, and the Scriptures form a central part of worship, one understands why Jews have always insisted upon a rigorous religious educational program for their children, which includes the mastery of the reading, writing and comprehension of the Hebrew language and its sacred literature.

VII

The Sabbath

The laws of nature help man to sharpen his understanding of time. Primitive men had little sense of history, and so their calendars reflected only the changing rhythm of the seasons. But early in Jewish thought we are confronted with a different and revolutionary idea. The Jews were not only interested in nature but also in history. They believed in God's sovereignty over the world of nature. But because they believed that God had created man, as well as the world, they were conscious of his guiding presence in the events that make up the life of men and nations.

Their festivals were, at first, celebrations linked to the natural order, and the dates were established by the life in nature. The Jewish month began with the new moon, and the dates of all festivals were determined by the phases of the moon. Thus, for example, Passover and the Feast of Booths coincide with the first full moon of spring and autumn, respectively. But to express their special interest in things that went beyond nature into history, they celebrated a holiday each week which was not determined by the natural order. This was their weekly Sabbath, given to man to teach him to reflect upon the meaning of human life. At first, the Sabbath was linked primarily to the significance of creation for human life. But it came to be a weekly reminder of the power of God to enter human history as the force that redeems. The Ten Commandments teach this most significant interpretation of the Sabbath day. The first time they are recorded, in the Book of Exodus, they explain the meaning of the Sabbath as a weekly memorial of creation: "For in six days the Lord made heaven and earth, the sea, and all that is in them, and rested on the seventh day; wherefore the Lord blessed the Sabbath day and hallowed it." But with the passage of years, a new meaning was added, as given in the Book of Deuteronomy, where the commandments are recorded for a second time: "And you shall remember that you were a servant in the land of Egypt, and the Lord your God brought you out thence by a mighty hand and an outstretched arm; therefore the Lord your God commanded you to keep the Sabbath day."

For this same reason, the festivals also came to have new meaning. They were no longer only a record of the passing of the seasons, as they once had been: they were now made to commemorate God's activity in history, as the redeemer and liberator. The history of the Jews might have been insignificant, if they were just another nation. But they considered themselves chosen by God to teach the world the meaning of his oneness. Therefore, they believed that what happened to them was important to everybody, because it was a demonstration of God's work in the world, through the people of Israel. Their history became sacred history; indeed, it was to become the very basis of their theology. Thus, the sacred calendar of the Jewish people is essentially a re-enactment of the historical events in the life of Israel. *Jewish celebrations of religious holidays are in-*

terpretations of the idea of God as the Redeemer in the living events of history.

Despite the fact that the Sabbath occurs with weekly regularity, it is the most significant of all Jewish religious commemorations, with the exception of the Day of Atonement. Indeed, in order to describe the special significance of the Day of Atonement as the most solemn of Jewish religious holy days, Scripture borrows the word "Sabbath" to highlight the extreme importance of that day and calls it the "Sabbath of Sabbaths." Virtually all the themes which are emphasized in the other major festivals find some echo in the Sabbath itself.

The essential significance of the Sabbath day is summed up in a single word—"holiness." In Hebrew Scripture the people of Israel are commanded over and over again: "You shall be holy!" And for this reason they are instructed to separate themselves from certain things, places, or foods which symbolize the profane aspects of human life. "Holiness" requires acts of separation; we must stand aside from the ordinary in order to achieve the extraordinary. The Sabbath is a holy day whose regimen of conduct is designed to set the Jews apart from mundane affairs, to sanctify a part of the week in order that the whole week may reflect a consecrated approach to life.

The Sabbath day, like all other days of the week in the Jewish calendar, begins at sundown the evening before. It is symbolically made to serve sacred purposes alone, with the recitation of a prayer of consecration at the beginning of the festive family meal on Friday evening. This prayer, known as *Kiddush,* sets aside the 24 hours that follow, for higher thought and spiritual reflection, for prayer, meditation, and learned study. In the *Kiddush,* which is recited over a brimful cup of wine, the symbol of bounty, there is reflected more than the concept of Sabbath peace alone; references are made to the liberation from the bondage of Egypt, as well as to the joys that come from the spirit of restfulness that descends upon the foregathered family.

Observant Jews do not perform any significant labors on the Sabbath day. In the morning they attend synagogue services, returning home for a festive noon luncheon which is accompanied by songs of praise and table hymns. The afternoon is often the time when families join in reading from sacred texts, discussing earnest and serious matters of human consequence. Before sunset, the afternoon prayers are recited, and they are followed by a "service of separation," known as *Havdalah*. It is as if the Jew has been endowed on the Sabbath day with an additional soul—an added measure of spirit and sweetness attends him. He takes his leave of the Sabbath with almost mournful sounds, for he knows that within a few hours he must return to the practical and material world, to the marketplace, the shop and the office.

As a sign of their love for the Sabbath and their eager anticipation of its return, Jews number the days of the week in terms of their proximity to the Sabbath day. Thus, Sunday is known as the first day of the week; there remain six days more for the arrival of the Sabbath—and so with Monday, the second day of the week, Tuesday the third day of the week, etc. Finally, when the evening of the sixth day arrives, the eve of the Sabbath, the religious Jew joyfully knows that the labors for the week have come to an end. And like the Almighty, as described in the first pages of the Book of Genesis, he looks upon all of his work during the preceding days as a prelude to a day of recreation. God rested on the seventh day from all the labors of creation, to teach man that the highest form of recreation is the spiritual rest and profound contemplation of the meaning of creation.

VIII

The Autumn Holidays

Rosh Ha-Shanah is the beginning of a period known as the High Holy Days. It ushers in "Ten Days of Penitence," that conclude with the year's most solemn day —the Day of Atonement. These days, while not "holy days" in themselves, do constitute a time when abstention from worldly pleasures and amusements helps prod the religious Jew to focus upon his inner life and to "take stock of the state of his soul." For Jews, the beginning of the year is not a time for hilarity and revelry, but rather a season of spiritual stock-taking devoted to the searching out of one's deeds and misdeeds during the year just concluded. These days are dedicated to God, who is sovereign in the life of men and nations.

In earlier Jewish history several different "New Years" were celebrated: The Royal New Year, for dating the reign of kings; the Tithal New Year, for reckoning tithes; and the "New Year for the Trees," for tree-planting time, still commemorated in Jewish congregations today with the eating of fruit grown in Israel. These were political, economic, or agricultural observances. Rosh Ha-Shanah was set apart as a high holy day, in the fall, to give the year a specifically religious beginning and thus set the spiritual mood for the months ahead.

Creation is the grand, universal motif underlying the colorful rituals and interesting ceremonials that make up the religious celebration of Rosh Ha-Shanah. "Today is the birthday of the world," runs the liturgy; "today, all of the creatures of the world stand in judgment before thee." So the prayers of Rosh Ha-Shanah are prayers spoken by Jews, not as Jews alone but as God's creatures, and not for Jews alone but for all of creation—for all nations and peoples.

On the New Year, the Book of Life is spread open before the Great Judge. On this day—some understand this literally, others metaphorically—all of the inhabitants of the world pass for judgment before the Creator, as sheep pass for examination before the shepherd. Three books of account are said to be opened on Rosh Ha-Shanah, wherein the fate of the wicked, the righteous, and those in between, is recorded. The names of the righteous are immediately inscribed and they are sealed "to live." The wicked are "blotted out of the Book of the Living." Those in between, are given a respite of ten days, from Rosh Ha-Shanah until Yom Kippur—time to repent of their evil ways and to seek the ways of righteousness.

On these days the setting and the spirit are different from the rest of the year. The Rabbi and cantor are traditionally robed in white, for white symbolizes the longing for purity of soul and body which is the theme of the season.

The music is penitential in character and the sublime prayers bespeak the significance of the moral life and the beauty of holiness. History seems to hover about the congregation as the worshippers reenact a ritual which goes back many centuries.

Perhaps it is this spirit of reverence for the ancient tradition which makes the blast of the *shofar*—a ram's horn—so climactic a part of the service. The service is punctuated one hundred times with the sound of the *shofar,* to the accompaniment of biblical verses which remind the congregation of Israel's covenant with the Lord. Why a ram's horn? The Bible lesson for Rosh Ha-Shanah suggests an answer: Abraham's faith was successfully tested when he showed himself ready at the divine command to sacrifice even Isaac; once the test was passed, a ram was sacrificed in Isaac's stead. The ram is thus the perennial reminder of the faithfulness of Abraham, and so it is used to recall to his people the faithfulness of the first man to seek the one God. The shrill, quivering notes of the horn are a call to action, reminding the Jew that the Kingdom of God must be sought in one's personal life, even in the midst of the evil of the world in which we live.

The ten-day penitential period moves toward its climax with the coming of the Eve of Atonement.

Yom Kippur, Day of Atonement

Yom Kippur, or the Day of Atonement, comes on the tenth day of Tishri, and it concludes the penitential season. This is the great fast day of the Jewish calendar, and it lasts for twenty-four hours. A public confession of all sins, committed wittingly or unwittingly, is the major theme of the synagogue services. Five separate and complete services, which begin on the evening of the Day of Atonement and end the next nightfall, make up the public observance of this solemn day. The first evening service is said at dusk by a fasting congregation. It is known as *Kol Nidre,* from its first words, which mean "all vows." The "vows" referred to in the *Kol Nidre* are only those which an individual has assumed for himself, voluntarily. Only those oaths of personal conscience, which a man has taken in his aspiration to achieve for himself a moral life, are involved. No promise, oath, or vow that affects the status of another person, a court of law, or a community is implied in this formula of absolution.

Yet, while the *Kol Nidre* serves as an absolution of ceremonial vows, and of oaths relating to religious rituals and customs, this constitutes but a single aspect of its meaning. It was undoubtedly originally introduced into the Atonement liturgy in order to emphasize the way in which a man must prepare for repentance. For, while ritual vows—those made between man and his God—may be annulled, the tradition specifically states that forgiveness for moral trespasses, those actions which encompass man in relationship with his fellowman, can be obtained only when the person who has been aggrieved pardons the offender. *The Mishna* states: "For transgressions between man and God, repentance brings atonement. For transgressions between man and man, Yom Kippur brings no atonement, until the injured party is appeased."

The *Kol Nidre* service has been called "the first movement of a devotional symphony which increases in momentum from minute to minute throughout the day." After the first evening service, the congregation returns home and early the next morning services are resumed. The four services that follow are so arranged that they may be continued until sunset without interruption.

The Great Fast Day comes to a close with the appearance of the first three stars. It has been a long day and there is weariness of body, but the people's spirits have been exalted. Buoyantly and expectantly they come to their feet as a long blast of the *shofar* marks the end of the fast. "Hear, O Israel, the Lord our God, the Lord is One," they sing out as one, echoing with fervor the monotheistic credo of their father, Abraham. And as the *shofar* is blown, from the lips of every worshipper comes the age-old longing, "May Jerusalem be rebuilt in the year to come!"

Sukkot, Feast of Tabernacles (Booths)

Five days after Yom Kippur, the first of the three harvest festivals is celebrated. This is the Feast of Tabernacles (Booths), or *Sukkot,* and it marks the change of moods from solemnity to joy. In the earliest period of Israel's history, it was known as the Feast of Ingathering, a week-long celebration over the joy of the fall harvest. Indeed, Governor William Bradford of Plymouth Colony patterned the first American Thanksgiving after this old Jewish tradition. But the three harvest festivals were given additional meaning in the course of time. The Feast of Tabernacles was made to signify the gratitude of Israel for God's providence during the forty years of wandering in the wilderness of Sinai. Like Passover and Pentecost, the other two harvest festivals, it came to be related to the major historical event in Israel's life—the redemption from Egypt.

The enriching of the purely agricultural festival of *Sukkot,* by making it into an historical and religious remembrance, was achieved by the Rabbis of the Talmud. They interpreted the "Booths," the ancient abodes of the Semites, to serve as a reminder of the dwellings of the Israelites when they wandered through the wilderness of Sinai on their journeys from Egypt to the Promised Land.

Thus, the Feast of Tabernacles became a logical sequel to Passover and Pentecost—the first commemorated the release from the bondage of Egypt, the second, the receiving of the Law at Sinai.

Outside of Israel, except among Reform Jews, *Sukkot* is celebrated for eight days. The first and last two days are commemorated by special services in the home and the synagogue. Devout Jews erect a small booth in which they eat their meals throughout the holiday, as a personal reminder of the hardships caused, in part, by the frail huts in which the Israelites dwelt during the years of wandering in the wilderness. The *Sukkah,* or booth, has improvised walls and a covering of leafy branches and twigs instead of a roof or ceiling. It must not be lower than five feet, nor higher than thirty, and it must be exposed to a view of the stars. Since the whole mood of the holiday must be re-experienced each year, a permanent *Sukkah* is prohibited.

The harvest side of the holiday is celebrated further by the ceremonial of the *lulav,* a cluster made up of a palm branch, three myrtle twigs, and two willow sprigs. The *lulav* is taken in the right hand, and in the left hand, a citron is placed. At certain portions of the service, they are moved to and fro: eastward, southward, westward, northward, upward and downward to symbolize the universal gratitude for the harvest, to the one God who is to be found everywhere. As the palm cluster is taken in hand, litanies of praise are sung, punctuated by the phrase "Hosana"—which literally means, in Hebrew, "O save us!" and which has entered the English language in Hebrew, untranslated, as "hosanna."

On the eighth day, immediately upon the conclusion of *Sukkot,* a one-day festival, known in the Bible as the "Eighth Day of Solemn Assembly," is commemorated. Special prayers for rain mark the services of the day. The long summer season of the land of Israel is over, the autumn harvest is in, and now, the people and the soil eagerly await the quenching and fructifying rains, which bring comfort and hope to both. Despite the fact that the people of Israel were not masters of their own land until recently, the special prayers of the synagogue established in the earlier days of their history kept sacred their ties to the Holy Land, and bound them to its soil.

Simhat Torah, Rejoicing in the Law

The very next day there follows a holiday which is not mentioned in the Bible, but which grew up in the Middle Ages. It is the day of "Rejoicing in the Torah," *Simhat Torah*. This is the time when the annual cycle of the public Torah reading is completed, and begun again. Exactly a year before, the weekly reading started with the first chapters of Genesis. Each week, thereafter, consecutive chapters of the Books of Genesis, Exodus, Leviticus, Numbers, and Deuteronomy are read. The services have been made to symbolize the eternal character of the Torah, and so the first chapters of Genesis are read immediately following. Thus, the cycle is never-ending. On this happy occasion, all of the men and children in the synagogue are called up to the reading, singly or in groups, and each one personally rejoices in the Torah. Joy stems from gratitude that God has enabled the congregation to complete and to begin another year of the study of the Torah.

On the eve of *Simhat Torah,* all but one of the Torah Scrolls are removed from the Holy Ark—the Ark must never be left completely empty of Scrolls.

These Scrolls are paraded in seven processions around the sanctuary by the male members of the congregation. Heading the "line of march" are usually the children who merrily wave flags inscribed in Hebrew with religious sentiments—various Scriptural verses.

On the following morning, the very last and the very first portions of the Pentateuch are read. The reading from Deuteronomy is awarded to a learned member of the congregation who is honorably called the "Bridegroom of the Torah"; the section read from Genesis is similarly awarded, and the man called to the desk for this reading is given the title, "Bridegroom of Genesis."

The Five Books of Moses, or the Pentateuch, are known as "The Scroll of the Torah" when they are written by hand on parchment and rolled as a scroll. The "Scroll" is, of course, written in Hebrew by a pious person known as a scribe. This scribe also writes the parchment strips contained in the *tephillin* and the *mezzuzah*. But his most arduous work, his labor of love, is reserved for the writing of a "Scroll of the Torah." This often takes as long as a year, for it must be done according to very careful prescriptions. In the synagogue, the "Scroll of the Torah" is wrapped in beautiful silk or velvet mantles, and ornamental silver crowns adorn its wooden rollers. When a Torah Scroll is presented to the congregation by a member or a friend, it is an occasion for great rejoicing. Each year, when *Simhat Torah* is celebrated, before the Torah reading the Scrolls are removed from the Holy Ark and carried in a happy procession amidst the joyful singing of prayers of thanksgiving. A gay, informal mood envelops the synagogue. For children, particularly, *Simhat Torah* is one of the most beloved of the Jewish festivals.

Hanukkah, the Feast of Dedication

Hanukkah, or the Feast of Dedication, the last of the autumn holidays in the Jewish calendar, is celebrated for eight days. Traditionally, it had been regarded as a minor festival, since it was established after the close of the Hebrew Bible. But in America, perhaps because of its proximity to Christmas, Jewish families go to great lengths to make this a joyous time for home festivities, and *Hanukkah* has been made into a most important religious celebration.

The events surrounding the story of *Hanukkah* are related to the victory of the Maccabees over the forces of Antiochus Epiphanes, in 165 B.C. This Syrian king, influenced by the dominant Hellenism of the day, had established a pagan altar in the Temple of Jerusalem, and the Jewish way of life was threatened with extinction by his anti-religious decrees. Judas the Maccabee led a small force of partisans, devoted followers whose spirit overwhelmed the outnumbering Syrian armies. They succeeded in reestablishing the Temple as a place of Jewish worship. Dedication ceremonies were held, lasting for eight days, following the example of those conducted at the time of the dedication of Solomon's Temple. From these ceremonies the appropriate symbol of light became associated with the observance of *Hanukkah* as the Feast of Dedication. In the days of Jesus, it was still customary for Jews to go up to Jerusalem at *Hanukkah* time. The New Testament writes: "It was the feast of the Dedication at Jerusalem; it was winter, and Jesus was walking in the temple, in the portico of Solomon" (John 10, 22). Indeed, the victory of the Maccabees had insured the continuity of the priestly tradition, making it possible for it to remain centered in the well-beloved Jerusalem Temple for over 200 years, until it finally fell to the besieging Roman legions in the year 70 of the Christian era.

In our days, at home and in the synagogue, a nine-branched candelabra is kindled—different from the one used as a synagogue symbol. With one candle the others are lighted, and each night the lights are increased until on the eighth and last light night, all nine candles are burning. A pleasant and intimate home ritual surrounds the lighting of the candelabra, or *Menorah,* and every night of the holiday season, parents and children join in the singing of religious hymns and the exchanging of gifts.

IX

The Winter Holidays

The Fifteenth of Shevat

Jews celebrate the beginning of the religious year in the fall, but they observe still another "New Year" in the winter season. In earlier times, when they still lived principally in Palestine, they set aside the fifteenth day of Shevat as the "New Year for the Trees." Even after they were exiled from their land, they continued to recall this ancient "arbor day," as a bond with their agricultural past. Throughout the lands of their dispersion, in the midst of European winters, when the fifteenth day of Shevat arrived, they recalled that spring was about to come to the land of Israel. It was a day of recollection and of hope. They recalled the land where their fathers once walked, where prophets and sages trod; they hoped that one day this land would again be theirs, even as it had been promised to Abraham. Although they used no rituals on this minor holiday, they symbolized their love for the Holy Land by eating Palestinian fruits and by recalling the agricultural life of the Jews in ancient Palestine.

That a Jew who lived in non-tropical countries should have thought of the coming of spring in a month like February, simply because spring was then about to come to Palestine, helps us to understand the close ties he maintained with the land of his fathers. Nor were these ties political or ecclesiastical. After the year 70 there was no Jewish state until the State of Israel came into being in 1948. There was no Temple in Jerusalem, either; the synagogue had followed the Jews wherever they went. But throughout the ages, the Jews retained a strong sense of attachment to the land that had cradled their people and which was the scene of the past glories of their heritage. On *Hamishah Asar Bi-Shevat,* the fifteenth day of Shevat, in Jewish homes, this sentiment still comes alive, and with it the land does, too.

Purim, the Feast of Lots

On *Simhat Torah,* Jews are happy because of the Torah. On the holiday of *Purim,* they recall with joy the downfall of Haman, their great oppressor.

The story of *Purim* is told in the Book of Esther, found in the third section of Hebrew Scripture. Mordecai and Esther are the heroes of the tale, which reads like a modern-day suspense story. Haman, vizier of King Ahasuerus, had plotted to kill all the Jews of the Persian empire. But the heroes saved the day. Haman was foiled and was hung from the very gallows he had prepared for Mordecai. He had chosen the fourteenth day of Adar as the day when he would annihilate all of the Jews of the empire. Instead of becoming a day of mourning it became a day of joy.

Purim is also known as the Feast of Lots, because Haman had selected the extermination date by casting lots.

This happy holiday is commemorated in the synagogue by the public reading of the Book of Esther both at the evening and morning service. The reading is customarily accompanied by the excited stamping of feet and the happy sounding of noisemakers at every mention of Haman's name. In many Jewish homes the day is also celebrated by a festive meal, highlighted by a masquerade consisting of the characters of the *Purim* story. *Purim* is thus a folk festival, sounding a note of light relief, and leavening the religious year with the elements of fun and merriment. It marks the close of the winter holidays for the Jew. Four weeks later spring will begin, when the dramatic holiday season of Passover arrives.

X

The Spring Holidays

Passover

The theme of Passover runs through all of Jewish religious life like a silver cord. Every Sabbath eve, during the prayers that accompany the festive meal, the Exodus from Egypt is recalled. And, again, on every major festival of the year, there is a remembrance of the wonderful deliverance which God wrought for the Israelites when he redeemed them from Egypt. The Jewish prayer book refers to this divine liberation from bondage many more times than it does to any other single event in Jewish history. For Judaism is a God-centered civilization and Passover celebrates God the redeemer. The redeeming God, for the Jew, is pure spirit, and his redemptive works are known through the events of history.

When the grip of winter is broken and nature is being resurrected, Passover comes. It is the first of the spring festivals, and on the night of spring's first full moon its celebration begins. Nature, too, is being released from its thralldom, even as the Israelites had gained their freedom from servitude. The new young grain pushing its head through the fertile earth is a reminder of life's rebirth.

With the two other harvest festivals, Tabernacles and Pentecost, Passover celebrates God in nature and in history. In the twelfth chapter of the Book of Exodus there is a detailed description of the manner in which the Passover was first celebrated. At the full moon of the first month of spring, every family slaughtered a lamb or a goat at twilight. In the middle of the night they ate it in common, together with unleavened bread and bitter herbs. The meal had to be eaten in haste, and whatever was not consumed had to be burned before the break of dawn. After the slaughtering, hyssop was dipped into the animal's blood, and a few drops were sprinkled with it on the doorposts of each house. This was known as the ceremony of *Pesach*, the paschal lamb. For a full week thereafter, a Festival of Un-leavened Bread was celebrated and no fermented food (*hametz*) was permitted to be eaten. In this way the early Israelites celebrated the first rites of spring.

But when they were liberated from Egypt, that great experience left an indelible mark upon their spirit. All the elements of these older ceremonies were now invested with the new meanings associated with liberation from Egyptian bondage. Passover now referred to the time that God "passed over" the houses of the Israelites when he came to destroy the Egyptian first-born. The unleavened bread became a memorial of the hurried departure from Egypt—there had been no time to wait for the dough to rise, and so the bread was baked without leavening. The historical significance of Passover as commemorating the Exodus, and its meaning as a festival of freedom, soon overtook the natural meanings of the older, agricultural phase of the holiday.

The Rabbis of the Talmud prescribed a number of regulations, based upon their interpretation of Scripture, which were designed to emphasize these new meanings. Jews were required to eat *matzah,* or unlea-vened bread, throughout the festival period, as a reminder of the bread of poverty which their ancestors had eaten when they were slaves in the land of Egypt. On Passover, the scrupulous avoidance of food that has come in contact with leavening or certain kinds of grain is also intended as a reminder of the food the Israelites ate when they were liberated. The motive behind these ritual precautions is principally educational: each Jewish home must relive the Exodus, so that it may come to know the greatness of God's redeeming powers. "For God did not redeem our ancestors alone, but us, as well," runs a prayer of the Passover home ritual. In this way, the Exodus becomes an ongoing process, for God's liberating power is unending.

This Jewish Feast of Unleavened Bread—*matzot*—has left its continuing marks on Christianity, as well. Easter was originally called "The Pascha"—and in some sections of Christendom it is still known by this Jewish reference. "The Pascha" associates Easter with *Pesach,* the paschal lamb offered by the ancient Israelites as their annual Passover-eve sacrifice. It is believed that the bread to which Jesus referred at the Last Supper was actually *matzah,* since it is presumed to have been a Passover meal eaten in Jerusalem at the time of the festival. Thus, at every Mass, the Jewish Passover is visually recalled by Roman Catholics, for the bread used as the host—the thin wafer—must always be unleavened.

Orthodox and Conservative Jews celebrate Passover for eight days, and the Reform group observes it for one week. But while major public services are conducted on the first and last two days of the festival, the Jewish home is the real center of Passover observance. On the first two evenings of the holiday, a special ritual meal known as a *Seder* (meaning "Order of Service") is conducted at the family table. Every member of the family participates in the ritual and is supplied with a copy of the Passover *haggadah,* a special prayer book containing the various ceremonies and readings connected with the celebration of the *Seder.* In the center of the table are placed the cakes of *matzah;* the bitter herbs; a roasted egg, to symbolize the ancient sacrifice; parsley, as a green sign of spring's coming; and a mixture of apples, nuts, wine and cinnamon called *haroset,* made to look like the mortar used by the Israelites as slave-builders of the store-cities of the Egyptian Pharaohs. At various points in the ritual meal, these foods are consumed and their symbolic meanings are explained. Many of these explanations are given with the children in mind, for they are very much a part of this family service. In response to the youngest child's "Four Questions," an old ritual formula having a pedagogical motivation, the father recounts the narrative story of the Exodus. The *Seder* concludes as all join in singing many joyous hymns. Passover helps to make the family, through its shared table ritual, into a warm and glowing community.

Shavuot, or Pentecost

The closing spring festival of the Jewish calendar falls seven weeks after the beginning of Passover, and is therefore known as *Shavuot,* or the Feast of Weeks. Because it falls on the fiftieth day following Passover, it has also come to be known as Pentecost, which in Greek means "fifty." The weeks which separate these two harvest festivals are called the "Days of the Omer," named after the Hebrew word meaning "sheaf." Sheaves of barley, the first crop to ripen, were offered as a Temple sacrifice on the second night of Passover. Thereafter, the farmers counted each day, expectantly waiting for the fiftieth day, at which time the major crops would be ready for harvesting. Then, on the fiftieth day, amidst great rejoicing, they brought the first pickings of their fruits and grains to the Temple, as another offering to God in gratitude for the bounty of their harvest.

During the time of the Rabbis, both the Days of the Omer and Pentecost underwent changes in meaning. The Omer days became a time of partial mourning, a kind of Lenten period. Marriages were not solemnized, new clothes could not be worn, hair could not be cut, nor was public entertainment permitted. Except for Sabbaths and new moons, some of these restrictions were lifted on only one day—the thirty-third day. The precise reasons for all of this are difficult to determine. Jewish tradition explains that the Omer days became days of partial mourning because of the plague which killed the disciples of Rabbi Akiba, a foremost scholar and teacher, and which abated only for one day—the thirty-third day. Orthodox Jews still observe this period in the traditional fashion, although most Conservative and Reform Jews do not.

The Rabbis reinterpreted the significance of Pentecost in a way that has been most important for Jewish religious life. Again we see how they understood the work of God in history. Their interpretation of the meaning of Pentecost hinges upon their understanding of the purposes of the Exodus. God did not deliver the Israelites from Egypt just to rescue them from bondage, important as that may have been. Liberation from Egypt was linked to a spiritual purpose. God freed Israel, so that as free men they could serve him. But how should Israel serve God, asked the Rabbis? The answer they gave is implied in the way they reinterpreted Pentecost. By revealing his law to them, God would teach Israel how to do his will. Thus, Pentecost became the great festival of Revelation, commemorating the giving of the law on Sinai. In the synagogue, this idea is highlighted in the scriptural lesson chosen for the holiday. From the Book of Exodus, chapters are read that describe the dramatic story of Mount Sinai and the promulgation of the Ten Commandments. In many congregations in America, as a link to the Torah, Pentecost has been selected as the day when Confirmation services are held for the graduates of the synagogue religious school.

As the spring cycle comes to a close, the Torah again becomes the center of Jewish life. Without the Torah, even the Exodus would be meaningless.

XI

The Summer Holidays

The Ninth Day of Av

The summer months of the Jewish calendar have relatively few days of ritual significance. The principal commemoration turns on the mournful remembrance of Jerusalem's destruction, and the loss of the Temple. Tradition records that the First Temple was destroyed in the 6th century B.C., on the ninth day of the month of Av. Some six hundred and fifty-five years later, the Romans destroyed the Second Temple on the very same date. Small wonder, then, that this date is observed in a spirit of mourning.

The observance of the "Ninth of Av" has been transformed from a single day into a season. Three weeks before it is reached, on the seventeenth of Tammuz, the mood is established. It was on the seventeenth day of Tammuz, that the Romans made the first breach in the Temple Walls, and this led to the final destruction three weeks later. During this three-week period, no marriages are solemnized by Orthodox or Conservative Rabbis, and public entertainment is avoided by traditional Jews. In the synagogue, on the three Sabbaths preceding the "Ninth of Av," selections that describe the impending doom of Jerusalem are read from the Prophets. When the eve of the fateful day finally comes, the synagogue is plunged into mourning. The veil before the Holy Ark is removed, and the synagogue reader, seated on a low stool as a mourner, chants the five chapters of the Book of Lamentations in dirge-like style. Traditional Jews fast for twenty-four hours from sunset to sunset, as a sign of their personal participation in the sorrows of Jewish history.

But soon consolation is offered. The seven Sabbaths preceding the Jewish New Year are known as the Sabbaths of Consolation, and on those days special consolatory sections are read from the Prophets. Thus, the season that follows the fast of the "Ninth of Av" is a hopeful preface to the New Year, offering solace and comfort.

When the New Year comes, the summer period has ended, and the fall cycle begins once again. In the fall of 1965, Jews welcomed the year 5,726. According to Jewish tradition, creation took place in September or October of 3761 B.C. To be sure, this calculation is not based upon scientific fact nor, for that matter, does it have any dogmatic sanction in Judaism. Rabbi Jose ben Halafta, a Palestinian Rabbi of the 2nd Christian century, had arrived at this calculation on the basis of knowledge then available to him. Since this time, Jews have followed his rather arbitrary figure as the basis for numbering their years. It is interesting to note, however, that Jews use the creation of the world as the starting point in the calendar, while Christians and Moslems reckon the years from the lifetime of the founders of their religions.

PART THREE

The Jewish Life:
From Cradle to Grave

XII

A Child Is Born

From cradle to grave a man's religion follows him. From time immemorial he has approached the significant days of his life with special feeling and concern. Birth, puberty, marriage and death are all such moments. Primitive man attempted to appease the wrath of the gods on such occasions by offering sacrifices of the most precious things he possessed; a child, an animal, or the bounties of his crop. With the passage of time the idea of ethical monotheism developed as a way of life for many peoples. But man continued to remain a man and not a god. He still felt the need of being a part of a power greater than himself. And this need was and is especially strong at moments of physical crisis when, despite all that man imagines he can accomplish on his own, he comes to recognize his own frailty. These crisis periods in human life are related to man's birth, growth, and death. That is why, although its customs will vary, every ancient or modern culture has developed special rites of significance that accompany man through these important moments of physical insecurity, *rites de passage*. Although related by the very nature of the physical crisis, the customs of each group vary. These differences teach us a great deal about the attitudes the group takes toward the whole of life.

For Jews, the synagogue is a sacred place, but not *the* sacred place. Above the synagogue is the law, and it reaches far beyond the synagogue walls. So it is that when a male child is born to a Jewish family, the rituals that accompany the first days of life take place outside of the synagogue. Jewish law, based upon Scripture, definitely prescribes: "And on the eighth day the flesh of his foreskin shall be circumcised." Whatever the origin of this rite, circumcision has been and still is one of the most basic of Jewish *mitzvot*. In Hebrew, this ritual is known as *b'rit,* and this means covenant or agreement. Its very name, therefore, suggests its deep meaning to the Jew. It signifies that from Abraham's time forward, the Jewish people believed that they had made a pact with God, to live in accordance with laws and beliefs that clearly marked them out as a separate people.

Circumcision is a sign of the covenant, and it serves as a religious initiation, on the eighth day after birth, into membership in the community of Israel. The rite is performed by a Jewish functionary, known as the *Mohel,* or circumciser, and it may take place at home, or in the hospital. The ritual of circumcision confers no new status upon a child born of a Jewish mother, nor does its omission deny such a child specific religious benefits. (A male child whose father is Jewish, but whose mother is not, would be required, according to Jewish law, to be circumcised, in order to be deemed Jewish.) At the time of the circumcision, the child is given a Hebrew name, usually one borne by some deceased relative. This is the name he will use whenever he participates in Jewish religious ceremonies which require it, such as Bar Mitzvah or marriage. Indeed, this ritual not only symbolizes the beginning of life, but also of a Jewish way of life. For, when the father recites a blessing of thanks for the privilege of inducting his child into the "covenant of Abraham," all the guests assembled at this festive occasion sound its theme. They recite together from the ritual: "As he entered the covenant, so may he live to study the Torah, to be wedded, and to live a life of good deeds."

The New Testament reminds us that Jesus, from birth, lived as a Jew. Luke writes: "And at the end of eight days when he was circumcised he was called Jesus, the name given by the angel before he was conceived in the womb" (Luke 2, 21). Indeed, New Year's Day—which falls eight days following Christmas—was always celebrated by Roman Catholics as the Feast of the Circumcision.

If the child is also the first-born son of his mother, still another ceremony is conducted when he is thirty-one days old. In early Jewish history, the law required that first-born males be dedicated to the service of God. They were Israel's first priests. Later, Aaron and his descendants were chosen to replace the first-born as priests. But a religious rite developed that required that first-born males, as a reminder of the role of their ancestors, undergo a "ritual of release" from their service to God on the thirty-first day of life. As Jesus had been circumcised, so was he offered up to God, by Mary and Joseph, at the Temple in Jerusalem. "And when the time came for her purification according to the law of Moses," the New Testament records, "they brought him up to Jerusalem to present him to the Lord (as it is written in the law of the Lord, 'Every male that opens the womb shall be called holy to the Lord') and to offer a sacrifice . . ." (Luke 2, 22-24).

In observant Jewish families this ceremony is still

conducted. A person, know as a *Kohen,* because he traces his lineage to the priestly family of Aaron, acts as the officiant. The father brings the baby before him and gains the child's "release," by making a symbolic gift offering to God, consisting of five "shekels." Generally, five silver dollar pieces are used. The *Kohen* then invokes the priestly blessing of Aaron upon the child and returns the five "shekels" to the parents, who then contribute the money to some charity. Today, this ceremony has lost its original meaning because there is no longer the institution of a priesthood in Judaism. However, many families still observe this rite as a reminder of the ancient laws, and as a bond to the historic ways of the Jewish people. Implied in the ceremony, too, is the idea that life comes from God, and children have only been "loaned" to their parents.

For new-born girls there is a simple ceremony which is conducted as part of the regular synagogue service. Special prayers for the well-being of the sick, or for personal gratitude on recovery from illness, are recited in the synagogue at the time the Torah is read. When this portion of the service is reached, the father of the girl is called to the reading desk, and after reciting the usual benediction over the Torah, he offers a special prayer for the health of the mother and child. They are not usually present at this service, for the father often will come to the synagogue on the very first Sabbath after the birth. As part of the special prayer, the girl is given a Hebrew name, and she, like a boy, will use it for religious ceremonies in the future. After the service, the happy event is celebrated at home by the family and their friends.

A child born to a Jewish mother is, by the very act of birth, already a Jew: he needs no further induction ceremony. The religious rites that follow his birth are not intended to confer upon him the status of a Jew as much as they are designed to symbolize the covenant of the Jew with the God of Israel. Abraham is considered to have been a Jew even before he made his covenant with God to serve him by becoming the father of his people. But the act of circumcision, which Abraham performed upon himself and the members of his family, inducted them into a relationship with God, individually and collectively, making his people into B'nai B'rith—the people of the covenant. Thus, from the very first days in the life of a Jew, his unique status as a member of a unique people is indelibly borne in upon him.

XIII

Growing Up

In the Hebrew Bible the age of responsibility is considered to be twenty. When a man reached that age he was thought to be an adult. But obviously, between his birth and maturity, some special ceremonies must have been celebrated. We do not know too much about what rites were performed during his teens. But beginning at least six hundred years ago, a religious event was observed during a boy's thirteenth year. This has come to be known as the *Bar Mitzvah,* when a boy becomes a child of the commandments. We shall see how this event is related to the blessings recited during the first days of his life, at the time of circumcision, when family and friends prayed: "May he live to study and observe the Torah."

From the day the child enters the religious school, his education consists of discovering what it means to be a member of the Jewish people. A basic part of this training deals with the law and the commandments, which provide the pattern for daily religious conduct. Until a boy is thirteen years of age, he is not responsible for observing all of these rules; his father bears the responsibility for him. But after he has been schooled in the religious ways of the Jewish people, he is expected to conduct his life in accordance with them.

The source of this special way of life stems from the Torah, and that is why, on his thirteenth birthday, the ceremony of *Bar Mitzvah* revolves about the Torah. On the day of his *Bar Mitzvah* he is called to the Torah for the first time, like any other adult male. Sometimes he acts as the reader of the congregation on that day and publicly chants the weekly Scriptural lesson. Most often, he will only read the weekly selection from the Prophets, or the *Haftarah*. The *Bar Mitzvah* ceremony almost always takes place at the Sabbath morning service, although it could conceivably be held at any service where the Torah is read. The Rabbi usually charges the boy with his new responsibilities after the young man has finished his ritual.

Since a Jewish boy reaches religious majority at the age of thirteen—for by then, he is expected to be literate in the law—thereafter he may be counted as one of the *minyan,* the quorum of ten males required for the conduct of public services. Yet the *Bar Mitzvah* ceremony is only a symbol of his new privilege, and even if a boy should not have performed these rites, if he is over thirteen, he is counted as a member of the congregation. Like all other Jewish rituals, *Bar Mitzvah* is not a sacrament, in which an inward, invisible change has taken place. It is a sign, a remembrance, and a symbol—but most of all, *Bar Mitzvah* is a status in Jewish life, and not merely a ceremonial. In the Jewish view, the change does not take place within the person, as such; rather it marks the age when a change occurs in his obligations vis-à-vis the commandments. Judaism insists that the actual performance of the deed, whether ritual or moral, in conformity with God's law, is the essential thing, and the practice of the law is based upon the fundamental requirement that the law be studied and understood. In a word: faith alone will not do; good works, studied and comprehended, give moral content and meaning to a man's faith.

Another of the privileges granted to a boy who has passed his thirteenth birthday, and of which the *Bar Mitzva*h ceremony is a symbol and reminder, is the right to don the *tephillin,* or phylacteries, during morning weekday prayers, at home or in the synagogue. This custom is based upon the biblical commandment: "And you shall bind them for a sign upon your hand and they shall be frontlets between your eyes." The phylacteries, like the *tallit,* were also part of the daily dress of Jews in ancient times, and later were adopted for ritual purposes, as a constant reminder of the commandments of God. The phylacteries consist of two small square boxes each with a long leather strap attached to it. One is worn on the head, the other on the biceps of the left arm, pointing to the heart—symbolic reminders that Jews must follow God's laws with all their hearts and minds.

In the head phylactery there are four strips of parchment, each in a separate compartment. Each contains biblical passages, written in Hebrew, which deal with some of the essentials of the faith: the liberation from the bondage of Egypt as a reminder of God, the Redeemer, and the basic "creed" of Judaism—"Hear, O Israel, the Lord our God, the Lord is One." In the phylactery of the arm these same passages are written on one piece of parchment. The Hebrew letter *shin* is stamped on the box of the head phylactery, the letter *yod* on the arm phylactery, and the strap of the headpiece is tied in the back into a knot shaped like the letter *dalet.* In Hebrew, these letters spell *shaddai*—Almighty—a suggestion that by wearing the *tephillin* each morning, the Jew is reminded of his duty to God. Indeed, the *tephillin* should be donned for prayer before one is permitted to eat: man's first responsibility each morning is to give thanks to God for the gift of life, and only then may he think of his own physical needs. Because the Sabbath and holy days are themselves day-long reminders of this duty, the *tephillin* are worn for prayers only on weekdays (Sundays, as well), but not on these other occasions.

We have been describing the way in which young Jewish men are inducted into their religious obligations, and no doubt the reader has been wondering why young women seem to have little or no share in these procedures. Actually, the early Rabbis who helped to mold these patterns were keenly aware of the fact that women play an important part in the religious life. It was their belief, however, that certain of the commandments were given to the men, others to the women. In practice, they developed an approach to the ritual in which the synagogue service, like that of the earlier Temple service, was conducted by men, while the religious life of the home was largely placed in the hands of the wife and mother. We will have occasion to see how this has helped to strengthen the life of the home throughout the ages. Nevertheless, in recent decades in America, there has developed a public ritual for girls in their twelfth or thirteenth year, known as *Bat Mitzvah,* or daughter of the commandment. In many Conservative and Reform congregations, where this ritual ceremony has been introduced, it has stimulated the interest of young girls in continuing their religious education. Now, they too come before the congregation and read a section of the Scripture, as a sign of their mastery of it and their allegiance to its principles.

A ceremony known as Confirmation is also held in most Reform and Conservative congregations, and even in certain Orthodox synagogues. Generally, it is held on or near the Feast of Weeks, *Shavuot,* which commemorates the giving of the law on Sinai. It is essentially a graduation exercise, signaling the completion of nine or ten years of elementary religious training, which culminates at age fifteen or sixteen. Here, too, as with *Bar Mitzvah* and *Bat Mitzvah,* the essential hallmark of the ritual for Jewish teenagers is intimately connected with the process of learning: the Torah and its laws are the essential thing. All hope for the continuance of the Jewish way of life is pinned upon it. To paraphrase Scripture, Judaism recognizes that "where there is no learning the people perish."

Thus, great stress is placed by all Jewish congregations upon the need for young people to continue their religious education long after the *Bar Mitzvah* and the Confirmation ceremony. Such educational programs require special effort on the part of teen-agers, who are already burdened with the full program of general studies in their public secondary schools. Yet, more and more of them are voluntarily taking Jewish religious courses, supplementary to their regular program of secular studies. In some congregations, provision is even made for special classes and seminars for young people of college age. Indeed, "adult education" is an area of religious programming into which many congregations are presently venturing, and with good results. In addition to courses in the Hebrew language and prayer book, adults attend lecture and study groups which reappraise the Bible and religious ideology on a more mature level than is possible in the childhood years.

Not in vain did the Rabbis of old teach: "The study of the law outweighs in importance all of the other commandments . . . for the illiterate man cannot be a pious man . . ."

XIV

Marriage

For Jews, the home is a most essential part of their religious practice. Despite the fact that many synagogue buildings were razed during the intolerant Middle Ages, Judaism remained alive, because the stage for so many of its sacred acts was in the home and not the synagogue building. For this reason, the Jewish ban on intermarriage is most strict. It is assumed that a "house divided cannot stand." And this is particularly true of a house like that of the Jews, where religion is so integral a part of daily living. Non-Jews may, of course, convert to Judaism prior to the wedding ceremony. Reform Rabbis require only a period of instruction for the convert, after which they will accept him as a full-fledged member of the Jewish people. Orthodox and Conservative Rabbis require, in addition, the traditional and historical rites: immersion in a pool of running water (*mikvah*) for the woman convert, and circumcision plus immersion for a man. In addition (perhaps originally because of the fear of possible physical dangers), there are forty-two kinds of relatives whom Jews may not marry. Other religious and civil groups have similarly banned what are called incestuous or consanguineous marriages.

Before we discuss the religious life of the Jewish

family, it is well that we learn something about the nature of Jewish marriage and examine the wedding ceremony itself. In Judaism, man's highest station is achieved through married life. Judaism begins with the basic conviction that since man is a creation of God, no element of his nature is inherently evil or sinful. That is why it frowns upon celibacy and has never regarded marriage as a concession to the weakness of human flesh. On the contrary, marriage is considered to be a sacred duty, a fundamental *mitzvah*. The Rabbis taught, with characteristic psychological insight: "He who reaches the age of twenty and does not marry, spends all his days in sin—or, at least, in the thought of sin."

Because it never recognized Greek dualism—the antagonism between body and soul—as a true picture of human nature, Judaism continued to insist upon the essential unity of man's nature. The body was not evil in itself, nor was it the source of evil. Man worships God with his body, as well as with his soul, the Rabbis taught. The first *mitzvah* in the Mosaic Law, they pointed out, was the commandment to "be fruitful and multiply" (Gen. 1, 28).

For these same reasons, Judaism came to regard divorce, not as a punishment for a crime, but as a frank recognition that the marriage was not fulfilling its sacred purposes. Just as marriage is integrally a part of the religious life, so is its dissolution; thus, in addition to the solemnizing of the wedding in accordance with Jewish ritual practice, Orthodox and Conservative Rabbis also require that a religious bill of divorce, called a *get*, be issued by a Rabbinical court once the civil decree is granted. The Reform Jewish practice in this matter parallels closely the contention of some of the early Protestant reformers that the laws of marriage and divorce and their regulation are purely secular affairs, to be regulated by the State. To be sure, there was some disagreement on the question of divorce among the early Rabbis. The school of Shammai ruled that divorce was prohibited except when adultery had been committed. The other school, that of gentle Hillel, whose views prevailed, permitted divorce on other grounds as well. The New Testament apparently adopted the view of Shammai, undoubtedly because such a view fitted in more closely with its understanding of human nature.

Because the home is so central in Judaism, it is actually symbolized at the Jewish wedding service itself. The ceremony may take place anywhere, and any learned Jew may perform it, although it has become the practice to restrict this right to Rabbis and cantors. But always, in a traditional ceremony, there is the marriage canopy, called a *huppah,* under which the participants stand. The canopy is the symbol of the home which this marriage is about to establish. As part of the ritual, the Rabbi offers the bride and the groom two cups of wine, the symbol of life's goodness. Wine will later by used in their home at virtually all religious occasions: it represents the gifts of God's bounties and their joy in sharing them. The ring is symbolic of the consummation of the marriage and of its sanctity. As the groom places it upon the bride's finger, he announces the meaning of the whole ceremony with these words: "Behold, you are *consecrated* unto me, with this ring, according to the laws of Moses and the people of Israel." He places the ring upon the forefinger because of its prominence. The bride wears a veil, a custom that also comes out of the same early background: for, among Semitic peoples, unmarried girls never appeared unveiled in public.

Only at the very end of the ceremony does she lift the veil, to indicate that she is now a married woman.

The various provisions for the man's maintenance of his wife and the mutual obligations both have toward each other are detailed in the marriage contract, called the *ketubah*. These include both the physical and spiritual needs of the man and his bride. Before the ceremony begins, this contract is witnessed by two men, neither of whom may be related to the bride or the groom. The officiating Rabbi, if not a relative, may act as one of these witnesses. The text of the *ketubah* was composed during the period when the vernacular of the Jews in Palestine was Aramaic, and it is still printed in that language as a link to the past. After the Rabbi reads the marriage contract in the original and in English translation, he, or the cantor, recites what are called the "Seven Benedictions." These are devoted to an expression of thanks to God for the institution of marriage and the family; for having implanted his image on the human race; and for the joy of the wedding and the happiness of the bride and the groom. One of these benedictions, in addition, offers a prayer for the restoration of Jerusalem. Ancient Jewish sentiment, based on Psalm 137, reminds the Jew to recall Jerusalem "above your chiefest joy." And that is why this prayer is included at such a supremely happy moment as the wedding service. For the same reason, the traditional ceremony concludes with the groom breaking a glass under his heel, to commemorate the destruction of Jerusalem. A Reform Jewish wedding ceremony will differ in a number of details. The canopy and the *ketubah* are generally omitted, as is the special prayer for the restoration of Jerusalem. Most of the service is in English, and invariably it is rendered by a Rabbi. For all Jews, however, marriage is a sacred act, and for that reason it is called *kiddushin,* or sanctification.

Like Jews, most other religious groups have strong feelings against intermarriage. It represents a grave risk of religious infidelity and, for the children of such a marriage, the serious possibility of being spiritual hybrids, rooted in no concrete religious tradition.

In earliest times, marriage was virtually a commercial act, necessary to the tribal economy, and woman was considered as a mere chattel. In Judaism and Christianity it has been elevated to an act of mutual consecration, which is related to the spiritual order of life. Indeed, if marriage is not sacred, then nothing else in life can ever be.

XV

The Family

Within a home where the Jewish religion is practiced you are sure to find a number of ritual objects that help establish the mood of reverence. None of these is a holy object in itself that confers sanctity or is worthy of veneration. Since Judaism is not a sacramental religion, it has no sacramentals. These ritual objects are there because they will be used as part of the various devotions that go into the making of the religious practices of the Jewish home. There is but one exception to this generalization. As you enter a Jewish home (or a public Jewish building), you will observe a small metal or wood object fastened to the right hand doorpost. This is a *mezzuzah*, within which is a parchment scroll containing, in Hebrew, the "Hear, O Israel. . . ." and the biblical verses which follow it. Through a little opening, the word *shaddai* (Almighty) is visible, the same Hebrew word mentioned in our discussion of the phylacteries. The *mezzuzah* is a denominating symbol, marking out the dwelling as a Jewish home, and reminding its occupants of the ideals and religious practices for which it should stand. The Bible commands: "You shall love the Lord your God, with all your heart, with all your soul, and with all your might." And it goes on to remind the Jew:

And these words which I command you this day, shall be upon your heart; and you shall teach them diligently unto your children and shall talk of them when you sit in your house, and when you walk by the way, and when you lie down and when you rise up. And you shall bind them for a sign upon your hand, and they shall be for frontlets between your eyes. *And you shall write them upon the doorposts of your house and upon your gates.*

The *mezzuzah,* then, is not a sacred object, and it is assigned no specific function in the performance of any ritual act. Its supreme purpose is to remind the members of the family to fulfill all their religious obligations both inside and outside of the home. And since these obligations are intended to bring the family to a closer intimacy with God, the *mezzuzah* has the Hebrew word *shaddai,* or "Almighty," placed upon it, as a constant reminder of this thought. Notice, however, that the reminder itself is in the form of a *word* and does not consist of a picture or a graven image.

Inside the home will be found the Sabbath candelabrum, which is kindled by the mother on Friday evenings at dusk. The Sabbath is greeted in the home amid blessings, pronounced over light, which are spoken by the mother. It is the woman who ushers in the spirit of peace and rest. When the Sabbath is over, light again is the symbol of its departure. A special braided candle, large enough to last a year or longer, is used for the home service of *havdalah,* or separation, said on Saturdays at nightfall. Sweet-smelling spices are also used as part of this ritual, as a symbol of the hope that the week about to begin may be a fragrant one. A special ritual spicebox is used for this ceremony. For the bread, over which the praise of God is recited by each person before the meal is begun, specially embroidered cloth covers are used. And for the wine, over which thanks are offered at both the Sabbath welcoming and departure services, as well as on other holidays, fine silver goblets are usually provided. The Sabbath is essentially a family affair, and it is celebrated by parents and children through these rituals.

The Jewish home also counts among its proud possessions other ritual objects which it uses on the sacred days of the religious year. There is the *Hanukkah Menorah,* the nine-branched candelabrum, used during the Feast of Lights in winter. And in many Jewish homes one will find an ornamental box for the *etrog,* or citron, which plays a prominent part in the ritual for the fall holiday of *Sukkot,* the Feast of Tabernacles. On this holiday, some families still erect a small booth in their backyard, adorning it with fruits and flowers of the season. They will take most of their meals inside the *Sukkah,* for the duration of the holiday, in remembrance of the biblical injunction: "You shall dwell in booths seven days . . ." (Lev. 23, 42).

For Passover, celebrated in the spring, a whole group of special items are kept. There is the *Seder* plate, which contains the ritual foods symbolical of the Passover Exodus. The *Seder,* or "Order of Service," is a home service, presided over by the father and attended by many relatives and guests. At the table, the drama of the liberation from Egypt is reenacted through biblical readings and ritual symbols. Only unleavened bread, or *matzah,* is eaten for the entire eight days which are celebrated by the Orthodox and Conservatives, or for the seven days observed by Reform Jews.

But what has diet to do with religion, one may ask? Observant Jews believe that it has a great deal to do with the spiritual life, as they understand it! While some may question this relationship between dietary practice and religion, closer examination of many other religions will reveal that special food habits are not restricted to Jews alone. "Man doth not live by bread alone," and he translates this idea into dramatic personal practices, through various self-disciplines. Fasting, for example, has entered Christianity via Judaism, and the various Christian practices which accompany the forty days of Lent, while not derived directly from Judaism, do reflect the Hebraic concepts that place food into the orbit of religious living.

But what are the special meanings which the Jewish dietary laws, the *kosher* laws, seek to convey? The answer to this question supplies a necessary insight into the value system of Judaism. But, before answering, a brief word is in order regarding the rules themselves.

There are no restrictions on vegetables and fruits, but among living creatures many species are forbidden. All winged insects and creeping things, which multiply quickly and are a pest to man, are prohibited. For fish to be fit, or *kosher,* they must have fins and scales; oysters, lobsters, and other shellfish are thus prohibited. Among the mammals, only those which have cloven hoofs and chew the cud are permitted; thus, virtually all wild animals are excluded. As for fowl, the Bible specifically lists the forbidden varieties among which are vultures, hawks, owls, pelicans, ravens, and storks.

The dietary rules also extend to the manner in which all warm-blooded animals are prepared for food. The slaughtering knife must be sharp, so as not to cause the animal any unnecessary pain. The animal must not be stunned before slaughtering, for this would prevent the free flow of blood, and the absorption of the blood into the meat makes the food prohibited. Only one expert in slaughtering who is observant of the laws of Jewish piety may perform this ritual act. He is a functionary of the Jewish community known as a *Shohet*, and he must receive authorization from a Rabbi. After slaughtering, the animal is examined in order to ascertain that there are no symptoms of communicable diseases, any of which would render it unfit for food. When the housewife prepares the meat for her home table, she salts it in order to let out as much blood as possible. Or, if the meat is to be broiled, the fire itself acts as the agent for the removal of blood.

There is still another dietary rule of significance. Three times Scripture records a rule against seething a kid in its mother's milk. According to Maimonides, a great medieval Rabbi and physician, this regulation was originally intended to extirpate an idolatrous practice, common among Israel's neighbors. It was later interpreted as prohibiting the cooking or eating of the meat of any warm-blooded animal with milk, butter, or cheese at the same meal. In addition, in order to avoid any possibility of mixing meat with milk, traditional Jewish homes use two sets of dishes, one of which is used only for meat foods, the other only for milk foods.

How do Jews understand these rules to be a contribution to their spiritual life? The laws of diet are intended to make the table an altar, not by a mysterious transition, but rather by making the daily acts of eating into sacred and sanctifying moments. If a creature's life must be taken in order to sustain human life, then, at least, let the physical act of eating be a religious act and not merely a carnivorous, cannibal-like performance! For such reasons, every meal is hallowed by moments of prayer, before and after one eats, and tradition-minded Jews will cover their heads for prayer at the dinner table, just as they do when they pray in the synagogue or at home. Indeed, every time a pious Jew places food in his mouth, he will recite an appropriate benediction of divine thanks; there are special blessings for bread, vegetables, fruit, wine, and even for water. Food, to the religious Jew, is a sign and a reminder of man's dependence on God, and his gratitude to the Almighty for the bounty of life.

Regarding the special rules prohibiting certain kinds of foods, it would be useless to speculate on the possible hygienic reasons for every one of their details, although many have tried to do so. Many of these regulations are undoubtedly the result of ancient practices and mores, the exact reason for which are not known to us. What is significant, however, is that they have been invested with religious meaning by being transformed into moral and educational acts. It should be pointed out that none of the animals considered fit for Jewish food is carnivorous. There is a moral meaning to this: carnivorous animals thrive on their acts of murder.

What is prohibited here is the enjoyment of food obtained through the continual destruction of living creatures. While one is permitted to kill for food, it is only a necessary evil, and the act of killing must be conducted in a way that will engender a religious mood. The *Shohet,* or ritual slaughterer, must be mindful of the non-righteous aspects of his work, and he therefore must kill the animal with the least amount of pain. Hunting animals for sport, and not for sustenance, is strictly prohibited by the Jewish tradition, in order to train men to resist any act which would turn them into parasites. Blood is considered to be the symbol of the life-force, "for the life of the flesh is in the blood"

(Lev. 17, 11). For this reason, every care is taken to extract as much blood as possible, in the slaughtering, and in the preparation of the animal for use as food at the table. Even eggs which have blood spots in them may not be eaten.

These regulations have played an extremely important part in molding the life of the Jewish family. Through them, the mother of each household has been given a special religious role in the conduct of religious life. Every time she prepares a meal, she is mindful that she is engaging in a Jewish religious act, and not merely feeding her family. Through her ministry, she helps develop a way of life in her home which her children perceive from their childhood on.

An ongoing series of religious activities permeates the entire household, and early in life these help the young Jew to establish a sense of loyalty to the Jewish faith. If in the past Jewish families defied many of the sociological trends of disorganization, it was the various home rituals that helped to constitute the "secret weapon" of the Jewish religious community.

XVI

Death

To the religious person death comes as part of the natural plan of life. It is inevitable, as everyone realizes. But to the truly devout, death is something to prepare for throughout life. To every religious man, death is not the end of life.

For these reasons, Jews, as well as other religious groups, face death with the assurances and the comfort afforded by the rites of their faith. Here again, as before, by observing what these rites are, we learn much about the beliefs they symbolize.

Acording to Jewish tradition, when a person is about to die he recites the *viddui,* or confession, a rite connected with the belief in life after death. In his last conscious moments he addresses these words to God:

> May it be your will to heal me completely. Yet, if it is determined that I die, I will accept it at your hand with love. Father of the fatherless and the Judge of the widow, protect my beloved ones . . .

His final words are those which stand at the center of all Jewish belief. "Hear, O Israel, the Lord our God, the Lord is One"—the unshakable affirmation of the unity of God and the world he has created.

Once death has come, the body is washed and dressed in linen shrouds. At one time in Jewish history, the wealthy were buried in costly garments. But Rabban Gamaliel II, a distinguished Rabbi and scholar who lived at the beginning of the second Christian century, asked that he be interred in a shroud similar to those used by the poor. Since that time, this custom has been adopted by traditional Jews, to stress the equality of all men. As a further demonstration of this idea, Jews should be buried in the simplest of coffins; expensive metal caskets are at variance with traditional Jewish procedure.

Some congregations permit the use of their own chapels for the funeral services of their own members. Usually, the funeral service is conducted in the synagogue only in the case of people who have made significant contributions to the religious life of the group. In earlier times, these services were held only in the home of the deceased, but in our day they are most often conducted in special establishments known as funeral chapels. A Rabbi usually leads the ritual, although there is no rigid order of service. Selections from appropriate Psalms are usually chosen, and an address of eulogy ordinarily follows. The service closes with a prayer for the repose of the soul of the deceased, which may also be repeated at the graveside. At the time of burial, the mourners recite a prayer of doxology, known as the *Kaddish*. This is the prayer which children will recite thrice daily at a synagogue service for eleven months following the death of their parents. This prayer extols the sovereignty of God in human life; it never mentions death. It is intended as a grand affirmation of God's majesty and beneficence in human life. Thus, the Jew is taught to thank God for the gift of life when physical life comes to an end.

Before the burial, close relatives make a slight tear in their clothes as a visible sign of mourning. This custom, known as *keriah,* or tearing, is based upon the biblical precedent of publicly rending one's garments at a time of death. The tear is made as the mourners stand erect, and they recite a blessing signifying their resolute resignation to God's justice: "Blessed are you, O Lord, our God, King of the Universe, who art the righteous Judge."

Immediately following the funeral, the family returns home to begin a whole week of private mourning. This period is known as *shivah,* or the "seven days" signifying the full week of mourning. During the week, the mourners do not engage in any gainful occupation, and they do not leave their homes, even for public prayers, except on the Sabbath. Instead, prayer services are conducted in the home, and often friends who have come to console the family will also participate. To be sure, if one's livelihood is at stake, he may return to work, even during the seven-day period. In addition, if it is impossible to gather the necessary ten men required for group worship, the mourners may leave their homes to attend the daily morning and evening services in the synagogue. The week is to be spent in quiet meditation, and a memorial lamp burns throughout this period. Often, the mourners will read such books as Job or Lamentations as spiritual aids in contemplating the significance of the tragedy that has come upon them. Mirrors, considered a sign of luxury, are covered over for the week's intense mourning.

Parents, sons and daughters, brothers and sisters, husbands or wives—only those close relatives are required to sit at home for the period of a week. After the week is concluded, they continue to show respect for the dead by not engaging in public forms of entertainment for another three weeks. In all, a full month, or thirty days of mourning in this manner, are required. Observant Jews follow this pattern of mourning for a whole year following the death of a parent, and on every anniversary of the parent's death, the family observes a solemn day of memorial, known as *Yahrzeit*. This is a German word, because the custom assumed its present form among German Jews. On that day, the male children make it a point to attend synagogue services, and at the conclusion of the prayers, they recite the *Kaddish*. A memorial lamp, similar to the one used during *shivah,* is kindled from sunset to sunset during the twenty-four hour period of this annual observance. In addition, public memorial services for the dead, known as *Yizkor* (remembrance) services, are conducted in the synagogue four times during the year, on the Day of Atonement and the three harvest festivals. Sometimes, before the end of the first year after death, a tombstone is erected over the grave. In addition to the usual inscription, it often carries the Hebrew names of the deceased and of his father. This is customary Jewish nomenclature, and can be traced back to biblical times. Thus Moses was known as Moses, the son of Amram.

The Jewish strategy of solace, if one may call it such, is intended to bring the mourner back into the community after a short period of withdrawal, so that he may find comfort through identification with the ideals of the group. From the moment his beloved is interred, the Jew is bound by strong ties to the synagogue and the congregation. When one of his parents dies, he will attend religious services at the synagogue for virtually a whole year, and during this time will come to see the needs of the community, as well as the sorrow of others like himself. Moreover, Judaism has arranged a kind of hierarchical order in the process of mourning, with well-arranged time steps. The first seven days after the burial are the days of most intense mourning, and there is much privacy during this period. But there is a gradual tapering off of that intensity of grief in the following thirty days, and in the next ten months. These are the days when personal grief is transcended through the synagogue, and the mourner learns the meaning of sorrow through spiritual service. Through his religious practices, as the days become weeks and the weeks months, the Jewish mourner may come to know the deepest meaning of Job's words; "The Lord has given and the Lord has taken away. Praised be the name of the Lord."

The wisdom of knowing how to face life and death may come slowly but it comes to many who learn to submerge their sorrows in the life of the group.

It comes, too, to those who know that in God's sight nothing precious is ever lost.

EPILOGUE

XVII

Man and God: Some Jewish Beliefs

As part of the public worship of most Christian Churches, the creeds which form the basis of their theological platforms are regularly recited. While all Christians share the Apostles' Creed many of the denominations have added their own confessions—for example, the Lutherans have the Augsburg Confession and the Presbyterians their Westminster Confession. The liturgy of the Churches is shaped and molded by their adherence to these special theological formulations. The creeds of the various Churches have become the foundation of the whole superstructure of their belief, because most Christian Churches and denominations originated as doctrinal associations of like-minded believers.

Some declaration of faith, some official credo, some specific articulation of belief marked these groups off, at the very outset of their historic careers, as uniquely differentiated from their neighbors. This explains why many of these movements, like Christianity itself, are named for their founders, who formulated a guiding set of theological principles in order to establish these groups as distinct from any others. Christianity is named for Christ; and so with Lutheranism, Calvinism, Zwinglianism, Wesleyanism, and many others.

At a synagogue service, however, one does not hear a recitation or public proclamation of *the Jewish creed*. The reason for this is simple: a single, official synagogue creed does not exist. Judaism, as its name suggests, is the religious civilization of *the Jewish people*—and congregants of a synagogue are more than members of a Church organized by a founder in order to propagate a particular theological formulation. For Jews did not adopt Judaism in the way in which Romans and others once converted to Christianity or, as one may today, adopt the religion of the Baptist Church after leaving another. Jews created Judaism—they were not converted to it. They molded and shaped a way of life, belief, and practice which grew organically out of their group life—and this has come to be known as Judaism. And so, while Judaism has its own unique attitudes about God, its theological systems have never been compactly or officially ordered, arranged, or defined. Judaism has been relatively free from the theological authority of a central religious body, and Jews have been privileged to enjoy wide latitude in defining and crystallizing their concepts of God.

While Judaism is often described as a religion of ethical monotheism, it is even more properly understood as a way of life based upon a Jewish system of *monotheistic ethics*. The law, or Torah, contains the essential precepts whereby the Jew is helped to know God—not by abstract or mystical faith alone, but rather through a serious attempt to conform to the divine plan for human behavior. These commandments, we have seen, are 613 in number and they run the gamut of personal, interpersonal, and social relations. While logically a belief in a God who reveals his will to man is at the core of this system, the Rabbinic compilers of the 613 biblical precepts nowhere listed "belief in God" as one of them. They understood "belief" in the peculiarly Jewish meaning of the word; no man could be commanded to believe abstractly and no human tribunal could punish him for not believing. The Jew accepts "God's Kingdom" by building it on earth.

In Judaism's view, the Kingdom of God (*malchut shamayim*) is definitely of *this* world, and man's tasks and responsibilities are centered *here*. The Hebrew word for "kingdom" (*malchut*) does not imply spatial, or political territory; it is neither a place, nor a world. Indeed, we truly absorb its original significance if, instead of using the word "kingdom" we substitute "kingship," or "sovereignty." It did not regard the establishment of the Kingdom of God as a supernatural event which will come to pass when this world withers away and the future world, the hereafter, is divinely ushered in. In Judaism, the Kingdom, or Sovereignty of God is realized with the establishment of the Good Society. Thus, the Rabbis saw God as more concerned that men should follow his law, than that they should mystically long to commune with him.

But the indivisible unity of God is the cornerstone of Jewish faith. If Judaism may be said to have a dogmatic theological position, it would certainly rest upon this principal religious conviction. While every generation in Jewish history was free to embellish this basic "dogma" in ways which reflected current concerns, the fundamental principle remained unchanged and uncompromised. Maimonides, 12th-century Jewish physician and Rabbi, clearly delineated the classical Jewish view when he said: "I believe with perfect faith that the Creator, blessed be his name, has no bodily form, and that no form can represent him."

The complete spirituality of God, the utter impossibility of imagining him in corporeal form, has resulted in a number of specifically Jewish patterns of worship, of important "do's" and "don'ts," which find their way into synagogue life. The so-called "pictureless barrenness" of Jewish congregations, in which the human form may not be graphically portrayed; is a reflection of the disinclination of Judaism to suggest, even remotely, that God has become man, or that man has become God. No men, therefore, have been elevated to the rank of saints in Judaism, for fear that they may be venerated in a way which should be reserved only for God. Even Moses, lawgiver and leader of the Exodus, is accorded no supra-human status by Jews. Indeed, his name has been significantly omitted from the Passover *haggadah*, and the redemption of the Israelites from Egypt is commemorated each year without so much as a pause to give special mention to the man who led the line of march toward freedom. Again, emphasis is placed upon God as the Redeemer, who does not become incarnate in any man—not even in Moses. In like fashion, none of the festivals of the Hebrew calendar glorify the persons of any of the heroes of Jewish history. Always, attention is turned away from the human and transient characters who filled the stage of past events, and who were, in effect, only playing a temporary role in the divine drama.

Resurrection and Immortality

If one were to seek a report in the Hebrew Bible of the afterlife of the great ones—like Abraham, Isaac, Jacob, Moses, Aaron, David, and Solomon—his search would be in vain. In the words of one scholar, "Death is a matter of comparative indifference in the Old Testament. Life goes on, and death cannot seriously retard its progress through the centuries of history." It is clear that in the Judaism of the Bible serious efforts must have been made to move the attention of man away from preoccupations with death and the dead, from necromancy and spirit divinations, and from the rites of ancestor-worship.

Sometime around the beginning of the Christian era, concepts of resurrection and immortality, popular among the peoples of the Near East, entered into Rabbinic Judaism. Theretofore, longings for immortal life among the Jews had been satisfied by the belief that the individual would find his fulfillment by merging his personal destiny with the immortal life of his people. Now, the Rabbis adopted a message: a promise of a happy ending following man's earthly existence—in time and in eternity. But they never rejected this world in their acceptance of another world—they *embraced both!*

By immortality, the Rabbis were suggesting that human personality has a significance that transcends man's flesh and that survives material decay and death. Man is endowed with consciousness, he possesses moral capacities—he has a soul! Just what happens to man's soul was never agreed on in full or final form, but a wide variety of theological opinion was expressed by different Rabbis. Similarly with the Rabbinic doctrine of resurrection: Some day in the future, the bodies of the dead of all time will rise from their graves, the souls will be called forth from whatever places or states to which they have been committed, and both will be made one again. Yet, here again, the exact manner, duration, and form of this otherworldly physical-spiritual reunion was imagined in different ways, by different Rabbis.

Nor was it easy to find clear biblical warrant for

such otherworldly concepts. On the contrary—scattered throughout the Scriptures are thoughts which seem to deny these: "The heavens are the Lord's heavens, but the earth he has given to the sons of men. The dead do not praise the Lord, nor do any that go down into silence. But we will bless the Lord from this time forth and evermore" (Ps. 115, 16-18).

The strong emphasis upon the Torah as the *living* Torah—a way of *life*—and not as a preamble or key to *life after death* remained predominant, even when the doctrines of resurrection and immortality were given sanction by the Rabbis. Thus, the details and forms of the hereafter—of heaven and hell—were never officially spelled out, and individual Jews were given free reign to interpret these broadly or narrowly, as their private judgment saw fit. Over-speculation upon the life hereafter, it was feared by the Rabbis, might lead to an obsession with the mysteries of otherworldliness; therefore they continued to teach that "better is one hour of repentance and good works in this world than the whole life of the world to come." While recognizing a belief in doctrines of resurrection and immortality, the Rabbis, nevertheless, continued to place religious emphasis upon this world—to make this earth and this society a good and congenial abode for both the body and the spirit of man. Literal concepts of heaven or hell were discouraged, and as a result, many Jews came to think of them in allegorical rather than concrete terms.

What is generally agreed upon is the belief that death is not the end of life—man's soul is immortal and in the spiritual realms of the Infinite, men live on. Jewish theology, however, is relatively agnostic as to the actual nature of the world to come, and generally is willing to leave the question to God for final resolution.

Since Judaism does not rise or fall as it vindicates or fails to justify this belief, its leading thinkers have never been preoccupied with problems connected with after-life. They have a basic faith that in God's universe nothing precious is ever lost, but beyond this fundamental conviction they have never officially elaborated a final and complete system of other worldly salvation.

Sin

The ceremonials and rituals which take place in the synagogue or the Jewish home are symbols reminiscent of the covenant God made with Israel. They are visible memorials of a history in which God chose them to be the Messiah-people, the moral and religious teachers of mankind. But Jews do not regard these as sacraments for they do not believe that "beliefs," or symbols of beliefs, can save man. Therefore, in Judaism there are no ceremonial acts whose performance bestows supernatural grace or endows man with the saving power of the divine.

But why does Judaism insist that there are no beliefs which in themselves can save? The answer to this question hinges on the problem of Original Sin and the manner in which Judaism views essential human nature. The Jewish religion centers its message upon the need to fulfill the law and the commandments because it applies itself primarily to the challenge of helping men to face up to and overcome their *specific* errors and their *individual* misdeeds. The Confessional of the Day of Atonement, therefore, summons Jews to a direct and explicit confrontation with these ethical and religious sins, by enumerating them, one by one. In the ancient Temple, moreover, no sacrifices were required of them to expiate Original Sin, for Hebrew Scriptures

did not require atonement for an inherited burden of
evil. Emphasis is placed principally on the human possibility of doing good. Scripture sums up this attitude:
"And now, Israel, what does the Lord require of you,
but to revere the Lord your God, to walk in his ways,
to love him, to serve the Lord your God with all your
heart and with all your soul and to keep the commandments and statutes of the Lord which I command you
this day for your good?" (Deut. 10, 12-13).

To be sure, Judaism is no Pollyanna looking at the
world through rose-colored glasses. It recognizes that
man does sin, being aware of his *evil inclination* (*yetzer ha-ra*), even from the time of his youth (Gen. 8,
21). Indeed, a generation that has seen the wanton
slaughter by Hitler and his cohorts of six million Jews
—*one-third* of its total numbers—surely is poignantly
aware of the reality of human evil. But Judaism is
equally mindful of man's *good inclination* (*yetzer ha-
tov*) and the religious accent is always upon his possible repentance—which it understands as man's return,
even until the last moment of his life. To make this
point abundantly clear, the Rabbis selected the Book of
Jonah as the special scriptural reading for the afternoon service of the Day of Atonement. In that classical
gem of universalistic thought, Jews were reminded that
God awaits the return of all people—even the people
of Nineveh, who had oppressed Israel—and offers
them forgiveness only if they leave their unjust ways
and accept the moral law of God. And thus of Nineveh, ancient symbol of urban wickedness, the Book of
Jonah can say: "And God saw their *works,* that they
turned from their *evil way;* and God repented of the
evil, which he said he would do unto them; and he did
it not" (Jonah 3, 10). This is in keeping with other
scriptural teachings. Says Isaiah: "Let the wicked man

forsake his way and the bad man his plans, and let him return to the Lord, and he will have mercy upon him" (55, 7). And Ezekiel agrees: "As I live, saith the Lord, I do not desire the death of the wicked man, but that the wicked man turn from his evil way and live" (33, 11).

Repentance, in Judaism, is based essentially upon a moral decision—to return to the law of God, and the abandonment of evil deeds and intentions. It is linked to a radical change of personal conduct and motivations. Thus, the Rabbis of the Talmud set up nine days that intervene between Rosh Ha-Shanah and Yom Kippur—which they took from the nine exhortations God utters in the first chapter of Isaiah: "Wash you, make you pure, remove the evil of your misdeeds from before my eyes, cease doing evil, learn to do well, seek after justice, relieve the oppressed, do justice to the orphan, take up the cause of the widow." What is written after this, the Rabbis queried? And, quoting further, they replied: "Come now, let us argue the matter, saith the Lord: if your sins be like scarlet, they shall become white as snow." In the view of the Rabbis, then, the *moral* reformation which the prophet Isaiah demanded of the whole people was made into the very means whereby each individual who had sinned could achieve religious regeneration, by a combination of his own will and God's mercy.

In Judaism, in a profound sense, then, faith is centered not only in God, but also in man. From the very opening chapter of the Book of Genesis, the outlook is one of moral and cosmic optimism: "God saw all that he had made, and behold, it was very good" (Gen. 1, 31). This basic affirmation is pronounced over and again throughout the annals of Jewish thought, across the years. Sin and evil are dealt with realistically, yet without morbidity. They exist and partake of the work of the Creator, but they, too, are capable of serving a moral purpose in life. Essentially, Judaism does not deal with the mysterious meaning of evil by suggesting a theological retreat from life's problems in an escape to a perfect world to come. Characteristically, in Hebrew, *mussar*—the word for "suffering"—is synonymous with "moral instruction." What we do with the evils which beset us—the moral lessons we learn from them—spell out, perhaps, the very purpose of sin and suffering in the world.

In Judaism, belief in God is demonstrated by living in accordance with his moral law: a man's spiritual life is not completely comprehended by his faith; it only begins with faith. From faith, Jewish teachers believe, he must go on to the fulfillment of faith—to a life of ethical conduct based upon the law.

God's Justice and Love

Very often, however, the Jewish concept of law has been misunderstood to include only the justice and not the mercy and love of God. Closer to the truth is the fact that in Judaism God is both just *and* merciful. He is a righteous God, and a loving God, at one and the same time. This is the "law"—the Torah—and the equating of this "law" or teaching" of Judaism with a stern, wrathful, immutable, and untempered justice is neither correct nor objective.

At the daily synagogue services, passages from the Bible are read which speak of God as a God of love and mercy: "Thou, O Lord, art a God full of compassion and gracious; slow to anger and plenteous in mercy and truth (Ps. 86, 15)." "O give thanks unto the Lord, for he is good; for his mercy endureth forever" (Ps. 136). "The Lord is good to all; and his tender love is over all his works . . . The Lord upholdeth all that fall; and raiseth up all those that are bowed down . . . The Lord is nigh unto all them that call upon him; to all who call upon him in truth . . ." (Ps. 145). Indeed, scarcely a page of the *Siddur,* the Hebrew prayer book, does not include some reference to the dual attributes—justice and love—by which the God of Israel is known and worshipped in the synagogue.

In dealing with this question, reference should be made to the manner in which the ancient Hebrew law of "an eye for an eye" has been both misunderstood and misappropriated. Long before Shakespeare's "Merchant of Venice" characterized Shylock as exacting his "pound of flesh," some referred to this as a Hebrew law of retaliation (*lex talionis*) and made it serve as an example of the cruelty and barbarism they saw in "the Jewish concept of justice."

Three basic pieces of data are necessary, however, in order to view history with proper perspective. First, the Hebrew law of "an eye for an eye" was, in fact, a great social and legal advance in its time. Other ancient peoples viewed such offenses as capital crimes. They did not requite an *"eye* for an *eye,"* and *"arm* for an *arm,"* or a *"tooth* for a *tooth."* In their "legal systems," they demanded a *life* for an *eye,* an *arm,* or a *tooth*!

Second, there is literary evidence to indicate that the biblical law was interpreted—surely by the Pharisees, but perhaps even before their time—to imply a legal principle of damages, rather than an act of physical retaliation. In other words, in actuality, the law was used as a guide for practical application: the *value* of an eye; the guilty one had to pay the injured man a fair indemnity for the loss of one of his limbs or bodily organs.

Finally, it is highly questionable whether, throughout the history of organized Rabbinical religious courts in Palestine, any capital crimes which came before them for judgment were indeed punished by the death sentence—although the biblical warrant of a "life for a life" made this permissive. The Pharisees put down legal conditions in cases dealing with capital crimes, with which it was virtually impossible to comply. To cite but one example: If the twenty-three Rabbi-judges who made up the tribunal voted unanimously to apply the death sentence, it was ruled that the defendant must be *acquitted!* How so? It was felt that if no extenuating circumstances could be found by *just one* of the twenty-three judges, the trial must have been carried out with a willful prejudice against the defendant! Perhaps this is why the Rabbis of the Talmud were quoted as saying that a tribunal dealing in capital crimes which meted out the death sentence *"once in seventy years,* is called a court of violence and destruction."

Now, perhaps, it will be better understood why the Pharisees interpreted the two Hebrew names by which God is known in the Bible in the special way in which they did. The two primary names for God, in Scripture, are *YHVH* (*Yahweh*) and *Elohim.* Interpreting the verse in Genesis (2, 4), "In the day that the Lord God [*YHVH, Elohim*] made heaven and earth," the Talmud said, "to what may this be compared? It may be compared to a king who had empty glasses. He said: If I pour hot water into them they will crack; if I pour cold water into them they will also crack! What did the king do? He mixed the hot and the cold water together and poured it into them and they did not crack. Even so did the Holy One, blessed be he, say: If I create the world on the basis of the attribute of mercy alone, the world's sins will multiply greatly . . . If I create it on the basis of the attribute of justice alone, how could the world endure? Therefore, I will create it with both the attributes of mercy and justice, and may it endure!" Thus did the Pharisees understand God to possess both the attributes of justice (*middat ha-din*) *and* mercy (*middat ha-ra-hamim*) as *YHVH* and as *Elohim*.

And yet, while the Rabbis of the Talmud spoke of these two attributes of God, the tendency in Judaism from the time of Maimonides on has been to desist from speculating too much on what God *is*. Maimonides and his fellow medieval Jewish philosophers were most reluctant to describe God in terms of human attributes at all. They felt that a pure monotheism could not support a definition of God which tended to humanize or personify him. All that man can really know about God, they taught, is what he is *not*. Any ascription to God of positive attributes would result, they believe, in a dilution of Judaism's highly spiritualized theology; it would lead to a materialization of the Infinite. God, in relation to man, is so transcendent, so totally other, that for man to know him completely, man would have to possess divine qualities. It is more important, they taught, for man to try to understand *what God does, not what God is*. In this sense, they were not speculative philosophers, as much as religious existentialists, who were concerned with the moral and humane effects which an exalted monotheism might engender in the life of the active believer.

The Messiah

What man does, in God's name, is the major preoccupation of Jewish theology. Even the idea of the Messiah, which of course was first enunciated by the Hebrew prophets, is considered by many Jews to have a meaning that is related to man's life on this earth.

Orthodox Jews, to be sure, still pray for the coming of the Messiah, and believe that the redemption of the world awaits his advent. Some imagine him as a mysterious superman, others, as an extraordinarily gifted leader of men and nations. All regard him as God's messenger, endowed with the power and authority to cleanse the world of its evil. While Orthodox Jews believe in a personal Messiah, it is a man, *not a God-man,* they mean. He will serve as the "anointed one," the King of Israel, will lead his people as the "light of the nations." The Messiah, they believe, will not come until Israel is restored to its place as the Messiah-people in the land of Israel, where their moral example may serve to remind the world of the teachings of the Lord. *Until the Messiah comes, Jews must surely remain Jews!* Indeed, they contend, he will not come until Jews become better Jews—until they scrupulously observe God's law and do his will, thus becoming worthy of the Messiah's advent. Then, the dead will be resurrected, Israel will be restored to its former glory, the land of Israel will again be alive to Jewish prophecy, and the days of universal peace will be ushered in.

Conservative and Reform Jews, by and large, do not accept the idea of a personal Messiah. They would contend that, in essence, the "Jewish Messiah idea" never centered primarily in the personality of the Messiah—he was a human symbol of the divine, but not himself divine. Rather, they say, Judaism was essentially concerned with the quality of *human* life that would be experienced in "The Days of the Messiah." Thus, they see Jewish Messianism as the provider of a distinctive Jewish theology: it helps to project mankind forward, toward a Golden Age yet to come. Most peoples have spoken of that age in the past tense; Jews provide the world with a belief in one that is yet to be.

The age to come, "The Days of the Messiah," need not necessarily be regarded as being outside history, but may even be possible within the time of man. God does not enter the life of man by becoming flesh, but he does enter the events of history. The Exodus from Egypt was not outside history, nor was the revelation at Sinai. While Conservative and Reform Jews no longer personalize the Messiah—perhaps because they fear that such envisagement could lead to a modern idolatry—they are impelled religiously by the hope that *men must labor together to bring about the Kingdom of God on earth.* Even the Orthodox Jew, who persists in personalizing the Messiah, still sees him only as "a righteous man ruling in the fear of the Lord"—his principal function being to help bring ethical perfection to the world. The progress of humanity, however, *does not depend upon him but upon humanity itself.* Jewish theology is inevitably earthbound and leads to the conclusion that in the long run, and *in this world,* God is going to be the winner, because man, whom he created in his image, can learn to repent of his evil ways and do good. This life can be transformed when man does God's will and welcomes him into the events of history.

The "Mission" of Judaism

Judaism, as interpreted by the Rabbis, holds that man can express his belief in God and in the vital meaning of the divine at work in the world, through a series of purely symbolic actions. Thus, many of the rituals and ceremonies were devised to give tangible and dramatic expression to Jewish God-belief. The Rabbis regarded life as a whole as a religious pageant alternating between moral actions and ritual forms, the purpose of which was to express the divine theme. Doctrines play a lesser role in Judaism, for it is a way of life based upon this Rabbinic system of piety rather than upon dogmatic formulations or mystical speculations.

Father J. Bonsirven, the noted French Jesuit scholar, has correctly assessed this aspect of Judaism. "Doctrines," he writes, "contained in Jewish theology are not expounded or even considered by themselves, as an end in themselves; they are all connected with living, and oriented toward practice. *Life itself, a rule of life, this is what chiefly interested every Jewish soul.* This is why, in their theodicy, the Jews scarcely thought of God in any other way than in his relations to his creatures. In their studies and preoccupations they gave chief place to what is concerned with living—wisdom was the science of life, of physical life quite as much as spiritual. And it was also inevitable that, in their teaching, practical directions took precedence, in numbers and almost in importance, over pure theory . . . It is in the domain of morals and religion that one sees most clearly the excellence of Judaism."

Yet, since Judaism does not actively seek converts, it has not been easy for Jews to explain to the world this essential religious purpose for their continued existence. This idea, however, needs to be stated, and it can be summarized as follows: a life dedicated to express in human action the basic belief that the world has moral meaning because there is a living God *is in itself a fulfillment of that meaning!* In the face of every old or new paganism and idolatry, Judaism has and will continue to regard it as its mission to proclaim to the world: God exists, life has moral purpose, and that purpose is God's purpose.

"You are my witnesses," the God of Scripture reminds Israel. To which the Rabbis of the Talmud added: "If you are my witnesses, I am God, but if you refuse to be my witness, then (so to speak) I am not God!"

Thus, the "mission" of Judaism remains: to keep alive, for all the world, the God who still speaks out of Sinai.

By never giving up their hold on this truth, Jews continue to serve as God's witnesses.

Glossary

Amidah: Literally, the "standing" prayer. This is the basic prayer of all services, and is so named because it is recited standing and in silent devotion.

Arba Kanfot: Literally, "four corners" (of a cloak). This is an undergarment with four fringes worn by observant Jews in compliance with Numbers 15, 37-41.

Aron Ha-Kodesh: The Holy Ark. In this Ark, placed on the east wall of the synagogue, are contained the Scrolls of the Law, used for the public reading at services.

Bar Mitzvah: Literally, "the son of the commandment." A Jewish boy who has reached the age of thirteen, who is henceforth obligated to fulfill religious duties as an adult.

Bat Mitzvah: A new ceremony, for girls of thirteen, which parallels the *Bar Mitzvah* for the boys.

Beth Hamidrash: Literally, "house of study." Study is one of the threefold functions of the synagogue; the other two are prayer and assembly.

B'nai B'rith: Literally, "sons of the covenant." Refers to the community of Israel.

Etrog: A citron, which, together with the palm branch

152

(*lulav*), forms the ceremonial cluster used in the Festival of *Sukkot*.

Gemara: A Rabbinic code compiled and edited in approximately the year 500 of the Christian era, based upon the earlier code, the *Mishna,* and the Bible law before it.

Get: An Aramaic word meaning "bill of divorce."

Haftarah: A selected portion from the Prophets of the Hebrew Bible read at the synagogue service after the weekly reading from the Pentateuch.

Haggadah: Literally, the "telling of the story." This is the ritual book that establishes the order of prayers and praises for the home celebration of the Passover festival meal, the *Seder*.

Halaka: The authorized and normative law of Jewish religious life, based principally upon the Mosaic law together with the post-biblical Rabbinic codes and interpretations.

Hemetz: Leaven. Foods containing leaven or coming in contact with leaven are prohibited to Jews during the Passover holiday (See Exodus 21, 15-20).

Hamishah Asar Bi-Shevat: The fifteenth day of the month of *Shevat*; celebrated as the "New Year for the Trees."

Hanukkah: Literally, "dedication." The Feast of Lights, celebrating the rededication of the Temple by the Maccabees.

Haroset: The mixture of nuts, wine, apple and cinnamon made to resemble the mortar and the "brick without straw" which the Israelites made in Egyptian bondage. This symbolical food is eaten at the Passover *Seder* meal.

Havdalah: Literally, "separation." The service which concludes the celebration of each Sabbath day, marking a division between the sacred and the profane.

Hazzan: The cantor, whose function it is to chant the Hebrew liturgy at the synagogue service.

Huppah: A wedding canopy. The celebrants at the wedding service—bride and groom—stand beneath a canopy which serves as a symbol of the home they are about to build.

Kaddish: Literally, "sanctification." The doxology recited especially in memory of the departed, by the mourners, at a synagogue service.

Keriah: Literally, "rending." The garment of the mourner is torn as a sign of mourning.

Ketubah: The religious marriage certificate containing the rights and duties husbands and wives have to each other.

Kiddush: Literally, "sanctification." The benediction of praise to God chanted over the cup of wine on Sabbath and festivals, declaring the sanctification of these holy days.

Kiddushin: Literally, "sanctification." This is the Hebrew word for the wedding ceremony, implying that the relationship established between man and wife must essentially be a *sacred* one.

Kohen: A priest. A descendant of the family of Aaron, who, in biblical times, were ministers in the ancient Sanctuary.

Kol Nidre: Literally, "all vows." This is the opening prayer of the Service on the Eve of Atonement. It has become well known primarily because of the haunting melody with which the words have become associated.

Kosher: Food that is ritually acceptable in accordance with Jewish religious practice.

Levi: The tribe of Levi, from whom the family of

Aaron was descended, acted in ancient times as the assistants to the priests in conducting the divine worship in the ancient Temple.

Lulav: The palm branch which, together with the myrtle leaves and the willow, forms the cluster that is used with the citron at services for the Festival of *Sukkot*.

Magen David: Literally, the "shield of David." Popularly, this refers to the six-pointed star—the Star of David—which is often identified as a denominating symbol of the Jewish people.

Malchut Shamayim: Literally, the "Kingdom of heaven." It refers to the sovereignty of God in human life.

Matzah (plural, *Matzot*): Unleavened cakes of bread used at the Festival of Passover as a symbolical reminder of the "bread of affliction" which Israelites ate at the time of their departure from Egypt.

Megillah: Literally, "a scroll." In the Hebrew Bible there are five books which are referred to as *Megillot* (plural). These include the following: the Book of Ecclesiastes, the Book of Esther, the Song of Songs, the Book of Ruth, and the Book of Lamentations.

Menorah: A seven-branched candlestick that was part of the religious symbolism of the ancient Temple, and that is also found in the modern synagogue.

Mezzuzah: A religious symbol placed upon the right doorposts of Jewish homes, containing passages from the Hebrew Bible, intended to remind the occupants of the sanctity of their dwelling.

Mikvah: A ritual bath maintained by observant Jews for purification purposes; also used by candidates for conversion to Judaism, as a ritual for admission.

Minyan: Literally, "number." A minyan or quorum of ten males above the age of thirteen is required for public Jewish worship. The plural, *minyanim,* is used in the sense of small congregations of worshippers.

Mishna: A Rabbinic code compiled approximately in the year 200 of the Christian era, and edited by Rabbi Judah the Patriarch.

Mitzvah (plural, *Mitzvot*): Literally, "a commandment." The Hebrew Bible consists of 613 *Mitzvot*—divine commandments which are intended to regulate the daily life of the Jewish people.

Mohel: One who performs the rite of circumcision. A *mohel* must be qualified by both piety and experience.

Ner Tamid: Literally, "eternal light." Above the Holy Ark, in every synagogue, a perpetual light is kindled to signify the continuity of faith. The light is never extinguished.

Parochet: The covering veil which is placed on the outside of the *Aron Ha-Kodesh.*

Pentateuch: The Five Books of Moses: Genesis, Exodus, Leviticus, Numbers, and Deuteronomy.

Pesach: Passover. The feast commemorating the Exodus from Egypt. One of the three harvest festivals.

Purim: Literally, "lots." The festival whose history is recorded in the Book of Esther.

Rosh Ha-Shanah: The New Year. This takes place in the fall of the year and is commemorated with special services in the synagogue where the *shofar,* the ram's horn, is blown to call the congregation to repentance —the theme of the New Year festival.

Sanhedrin: Literally, "synod." The ancient council of Rabbis that met in Jerusalem, and that had supreme authority in all matters dealing with Jewish law.

Seder: Literally, "order of service." The ritual meal conducted in Jewish homes on the first nights of the Passover.

Shaddai: Literally, "Almighty." A synonym for God, the

word "Shaddai" is placed in the center of a *Mezzuzah* and also forms the symbolism of the phylacteries. *Shaddai,* the Almighty, is thus the ever-present force in each Jewish home and is also recognized as the power that motivates all of life, each day.

Shavuot: Literally, "weeks." The Feast of Pentecost or Feast of Weeks occurs fifty days (seven weeks) after the second day of Passover.

Shema: An abbreviation of the Hebrew prayer, *Shema Yisrael*: Hear, O Israel, the Lord our God, the Lord is One.

Shivah: Literally, "a week." This denotes the period of seven days which mourners are required to observe. They withdraw from their usual pursuits, remaining at home for prayer and meditation immediately following the death of a close kin.

Shofar: A ram's horn. This is the instrument which is blown in the synagogue prior to the New Year and on the New Year itself. It is a reminder of the need for repentance and surrender to the will of God.

Shohet: One who slaughters animals or fowl according to Jewish ritual. He must be an observant Jew and must be certified by a Rabbi as proficient in the knowledge of laws pertaining to slaughter.

Shul: A synagogue.

Siddur: The order of Service. The compilation of prayers which has been assembled over the centuries and which comprises the Prayer Book of the Jewish congregation.

Sidrah (plural, *Sidrot*): The biblical "portion of the week." The Five Books of Moses have been divided into fifty-four "portions of the week" which are read in the synagogue throughout the year.

Simhat Torah: Literally, the "Rejoicing in the Law." This holiday is celebrated at the close of the Feast of

Tabernacles. The annual cycle of Torah reading is concluded and begun again.

Sukkah; (plural, *Sukkot*): The *Sukkah* is the hut which Jews erect during the Festival of Booths, and in which they take their meals, whenever possible, during the eight days of the holiday. It is erected to remind Jews of the primitive and frail abodes in which their ancestors dwelt during their forty years' wandering in the desert of Sinai.

Sukkot: The Feast of Tabernacles or Feast of Booths.

Tallit: A prayer shawl, worn by males at divine worship in the synagogue.

Talmud: The Talmud consists of both Rabbinic codes —*Mishna* and *Gemara*—and forms the basis of Jewish law compiled by the Rabbis in the post-biblical period.

Talmud Torah: An elementary school for Jewish religious education.

TaNak: The Hebrew Bible. *TaNak* represents the first letters of *Torah* (Pentateuch), *Neviim* (Prophets) and *Ketuvim* (Hagiographa)—the three divisions of Scripture.

Tephillin: Phylacteries. These consist of the head-phylactery and the arm-phylactery placed upon the head and arm, which Jewish males over the age of thirteen don for morning prayer each day—with the exception of Sabbath and Festivals.

Torah: In a limited sense the Five Books of Moses (Pentateuch). More broadly, Torah refers to all of Jewish learning and culture, both biblical and Rabbinic.

Tzitzit: Literally, "fringes." The Israelites were commanded to make fringes in the corners of their garments (see Numbers 15, 37-41).

Viddui: The "confession" recited by the dying.

Yahrzeit: The anniversary of the death of a near relative commemorated by means of special prayers at home and in the synagogue.

Yetzer Hara: The "evil inclination" of man's nature.

Yetzer Ha-tov: The "good inclination" of man's nature.

Yizkor: The memorial service recited by mourners, which forms part of the regular services of the synagogue on four occasions of the year: the Day of Atonement, and the Festivals of *Sukkot, Passover,* and *Shavuot.*

Yom Kippur: The Day of Atonement. This occurs ten days following the beginning of the Jewish New Year. It is observed as a solemn day by means of a twenty-four hour fast.